CULTURE OF ONE

CULTURE OF ONE

ALICE NOTLEY

PENGUIN POETS

PENGUIN BOOKS
Published by the Penguin Group
Penguin Group (USA) Inc., 375 Hudson Street, New York, New York 10014, U.S.A.
Penguin Group (Canada), 90 Eglinton Avenue East, Suite 700, Toronto, Ontario, Canada M4P 2Y3
(a division of Pearson Penguin Canada Inc.)
Penguin Books Ltd, 80 Strand, London WC2R 0RL, England
Penguin Ireland, 25 St Stephen's Green, Dublin 2, Ireland (a division of Penguin Books Ltd)
Penguin Group (Australia), 250 Camberwell Road, Camberwell, Victoria 3124, Australia (a division of
Pearson Australia Group Pty Ltd)
Penguin Books India Pvt Ltd, 11 Community Centre, Panchsheel Park, New Delhi – 110 017, India
Penguin Group (NZ), 67 Apollo Drive, Rosedale, North Shore 0632, New Zealand (a division of Pearson
New Zealand Ltd)
Penguin Books (South Africa) (Pty) Ltd, 24 Sturdee Avenue, Rosebank, Johannesburg 2196, South Africa

Penguin Books Ltd, Registered Offices:
80 Strand, London WC2R 0RL, England

First published in Penguin Books 2011

10 9 8 7 6 5 4 3 2 1

Page vii constitutes an extension of this copyright page.

ISBN 978-0-14-311893-0
CIP data available

Printed in the United States of America
Set in Adobe Jenson Pro
Designed by Ginger Legato

Some of these poems have been previously published in *The Pulchritudinous Review, Fence, Margie, Daedalus, Upstairs at Duroc,* and *Cock-Now Zine.*

In memory of Marie

CULTURE OF ONE

I

Down on Front Street

Once again at the beginning I am down on Front Street,
by the old drugstore, the pharmacy where all healing starts.
It's possible one begins in healing in mercy in self-kindness. Don't
you know this? I don't know anything. There's a sudden change
in the weather—three signals click click click. Because
it was too hot and stark, but now we can have a cloud, the most
necessary thing: some say it's for rain but I think not, it's
a cloud, it's itself, grey and luminous and sun-shielding. Do
you love it? I fear it, but I gradually wonder if I should. A vast and
silken entity, and one sees that it possesses tentacles, extensions,
silky grey arms hanging down. With a joyous look on his face a dark
man touches one of these arms—for the cloud is that close, it's in the street;
but I'm afraid and enter the pharmacy to watch the cloud from behind
the glass wall: should I go back outside and touch it? Eventually . . .

At the Beginning Stop Suffering

I am mercy; I have no understanding of who I am;
though, with my thousand arms, I have written of my own
nature since writing began. I inhabit you and you write about me again.
There is always the sound or color or feeling in which I can arrive.
Lying in bed suffering from loneliness or anger the woman
with eyes closed sees me bending over her, a many-armed figure
wearing a rayed disk hat. Not a clear image, but made of the blue and red
brocade beneath the eyelids. Yes you were right, you contain all
the qualities and possibilities, all the gods—I'm here inside when
you need me; I can come to you when you've forgotten my
name; a voice of yours, hidden to you, calls for mercy and mercy always comes.

The Mercy Moment

The most outstanding characteristic of the mercy moment, the time when she comes, is how instantly the suffering stops. You have to stop thinking. You don't have time for guilt, or you will neither sleep nor begin again. This was how I started this time; then I asked myself what I would like to read, or rather what items I wanted in my culture, to contain created, newly and justly, my needs. The world isn't a text to be deciphered, it is a new creation though ancient—but what is antiquity to me? Every moment must destroy suffering anew; a cloud enters you, to begin in.

The Acquisition of the Senses

They, too, wandered in darkness, crying out for a home in the body of mercy.
The Dark could not perceive its own form
It was not a silk to be worn. Did the Dark want to know itself?
This poem is for me, I said, I'm trying to know something.
With what? "With" is not valid. It isn't a universe of language,

Abruptly I turn and flee. You can't reduce me to my organs, I say.
Thus does Chaos maintain her secret, from which I now speak.
But I couldn't resist the senses shimmering against the black backdrop,
and I put them on. The equipment made me *look like something*,
I was located and so I might die. Though *not I*.

These robotic jewels can be stroked or focused.

Parts of my corpse are laid out on a table—Someone
has destroyed my work, reconstructing it as a person: it's *their*
definition of appearance. It was not so lustrous, layered, and smoky as I myself am.

But I have to appeal to the senses again, as if they were more than toys
in their present form. So I arise and paste on my eyes.

I Invented the Arts

I invented the arts to stay alive

The art of seeing one carries about a transformational or formational
tool the greens and blues the golds with which a lion or eagle was justly *seen*,
existent in me. A space in which raw maroon or red is invented, either first—

Marie sat with her dogs eating supper.
She had caught fish in the river drying up but the time had not yet
been completed of its sapphire malachite existence in motion a flowing band.

Far from the great city bisected by the river Seine.
An initial light trembling when the shape of mercy was made.
I have traveled very far and spoken in many idioms, an alien;

I entered the bureau and cried. They were trying to rename me again. My
greying hair was cut short. I wore jeans and a tight leather jacket someone had given
me. I shouted and cried before the woman who was in her way being kind: don't
try to change your civil state she said. And parenthetically you are an immigrant as
well as a woman, don't expect too much. I myself was very thin from my medical
treatment, but this is just one story.

It is a passionate world though—Why?

Eve Love

Eve Love wasn't even that smart:
You are the product of random seed, aren't you? Yet irreversible . . .
No I've always been alive. I had forgotten about her though

I had done something upsetting to others that was either right or wrong
Who did it? Not Eve Love. How do you know I'm
not Eve Love?
I couldn't control myself. Who couldn't control?
I trust my emotions, when I'm not making
them up but they hurt like hell.
Why should anyone go through so much in order to be treated right?

Eve Love will walk all over your story.
She is coming to wipe us out with love, so be wary.

What do you think about your incurable past?
I have bloody scabs on my thighs. I hadn't noticed them before
Eve Love showed them to me.
You should be crazy by now.

The problem is . . . and then glancing at her résumé he becomes rattled.

I was born in you, you were born in me.
We have had all the children together, of all the lands forever

I won't accept anything but your love.
I can find it inside your bizarre heart, with my pointy-nailed finger . . .
I'm ripping the plastic off the constrictive embroidery
I'm stabbing you right in the cherry, you cruel little shit.

The Mask

The mask is what you use; it isn't a fake, it's a mask. Your senses love you; they evolved to be your mask—or you made them, didn't you?

I keep talking to my future self: she tells me how to be her. I'm already her, that mask.

The bacterium put on its mask, a painstaking silver drop. The quail flies up, I see his red crest which is almost invisible in dawn and desert dun, don't alliterate or you'll go to hell.

In my culture I need to repeat sounds, so I can step across the instant gap to future, future her. I can't even know what I'll write, she tells me things.

Light through rabbit's ear orange-pink on other side of gully. The rabbit's mask's alien, but I can humanize him—he can be powerful and dangerous. The dark chaotic wind—not wind—can flash from his eye holes, and his teeth holes can be scary.

Why are you scared? Afraid you're going to die? Are you still afraid of that? she asks. It's not that she's smug. Even though she knows what's going to happen to me. But she's not dead yet either.

The mask is covered with writing that people think they understand, *now* they understand it; you never understood it. Before. *Now* you can.

The mask is leering at you, with its dark mouth and eyes: you can't understand what you're making up right now, so get on with making it up.

Purpose

I want the edges of this poem to be hazy on all four sides
without literally being that. Torn and blurred, or burnt.

Her mother's address had been unconditional, though she couldn't remember it
Mom could loom over you, enlightenment.

You cook it really slowly, you buy a couple of basters,
you can't remember how to say baster in French. There's never been any
point to being here, stepping into the future, in order to get past.
Mercy destroys all consequences, for a time.

Because it was never about being right, being alive: I lost
my place. They wanted me to teach a seminar in peacock analysis—
someone to control your mental needs, *we*
supply them as always. What a dumb situation on that shore,
Marie hummed. She smelled like dirt. These dogs are
pretty terrific and the moon howls at them.
Then my pencil gets blunt; a few more words—forgive . . . safe.

Overmodeled Skull

It can't see anything, doesn't want to. Doesn't have to says voice
you are anthropomorphic. Well, so the fuck what?
I have ocher blood all over my cheeks. I'm holding onto a baby lion,
hope it doesn't pee on me—it won't. I am arising
as a voice from the belly of the shark.

Some goddess is waging puling war in her dissertation style.

I'm too bizarre to go to school again. I
want to be scary, that's all. So I can make it down the street.

Your crotch still has power, with its tremendous frightening
slit—another mask. I don't have to
breathe or dream: not in this black void where I really am.

I've grown very tall and large, and may not fit into the métro.
Are you battling some demons? Only you my sweet

god I hate that vapid on exhibit form stuff.

Scratch your cheeks and face the humorless circumstance
no one's delighted to see you; it's a soft world, full of murders
committed for one by others. I'm not in it—I'm not here.

Then I Became Mercy

Then I became Mercy with her one thousand arms; they were all I was. All
over my front and from my back—I had no hidden thoughts. No time, it seemed,
for the Secret. The arms were the space of me: what was my face? I tried for a
delicate Korean aspect at first, but then I might as well be the cloud: am I the
cloud? I'm still not sure. Having the arms one scarcely sees what one does with
them. Obviously one cannot choose who one's merciful to, one doesn't even see
them! It's all arms, arms, arms. I think it works by my simply having the arms, they
are what you need; you touch one, and it's done. You've obtained mercy, which is
what? Cessation of your suffering for a time. How do I have this ability? All I can
say is that I accepted the arms, the arms themselves. It's contained in the leap from
not having the arms to having them. Once you have them, that's it.

Culture of One

Marie made things in the gully: she made her life, sure, more than practically anyone else did, but she wrote things down on paper discarded in the dump and she made figures out of wood and rocks and cord and burntness and whatever. The figures didn't really look like anyone, maybe her a little, and the dogs the same color as everything with wolf mouths, I mean coyote.

Every once in a while a kid burned down her shack, while she was out foraging. Then her works both written and made out of stuff would get burnt. She'd start again. She always remembered how to do it.

Where does culture come from? It comes from the materials you do it with.

When she made the shark out of rotting wood, I guess it was just a fish. A carp, probably; but she called it a shark. She put a little woman in its mouth, but it wasn't her; and it wasn't me, whatever I say. It was the wood calling out. It was just some woman, no it wasn't even a woman.

What are you going to do when they burn up your shack? I don't care, it'll still be great here.

Language of Mercy

They seem unapproachable in the crowded room—Tara and her father
at night: she'd *have* to be young and with him. And I'd *have* to owe
them tentativeness. But who set up this system of debts
sticking to you baby a lawyer's daydream—*My* culture won't have
a legal system. I'm still not sorry for everything I've done.

He's protecting his merciful child but she *is* mercy and needs no
protection. I don't need to be sorry, I need to be merciful.

Your hair is all in clumps; your future self forgives you
you mime paroxysms of grief in the vision: I don't want to feel
I don't want to feel any more today and prefer the symbolic world.
I have been living poems for so long I'm only a figure and I'm glad.

You opened this particular poem and you're inside, you can't
get out. Shall we talk about the origin of fear again?

Walk toward the gathering one more time, with its yellow
mound of disorder—a cloth perhaps—at one side of the area.
He thinks he has to protect her, but Mercy needs no protection,
and has no time for fear. Part of me chooses to be her.

Someone is singing to me; I suppose it's a prayer or invocation
Birds gather in the mesquite tree, confessing to existence.

Skull

I took a skull and transformed it. It looks like a
different one. I know it used to have ruby brains inside.
And dreams that I interpreted badly. And wretched onyx-hooked
and emerald-gush *feelings*. And the rattle of reasoning . . . conk, conk.
Take it out, and here's this skull, and you still think it talks like you,

famished my tongue casts about for a confirmative taste.

Then I know I'm the beautiful monster I've made. Naked bares
my fantasy teeth—so we can feel better. My errors could not
be forgiven by others; but now we're the color of lions and peacocks, we, I,

have painted tears, and real-bead brains. I mean literal birds
in my mouth. I'm what they call an overmodeled skull,

I have shiny seashells for eyes; I have lizard guts for hair.
I think the best thoughts I can imagine. I also receive them,
from nowhere, at all. I have a lot of voices, I spew them
they look like overmodeled snake nerves, sequins on fiber slime.
Actually she pastes them to me, so she can talk. She began
existing by doing this, fabricated cowrie-shell eons of light years ago.

Old Food

A woman stands in a dreamed cemetery where her daughter lies.
It was Marie; one of them was. A woman stands near a rectangular
plot marked off in pencil. Now the color deepens to turquoise.
Surrounded by dusty gold and calligraphy gone past its meaning.

Marie lived in a gully at the dump on the outskirts of town, in a palm-
frond shack, with her dogs. She walks to the Buy-Rite: past a real cemetery,
towards the tracks, but turns; she enters the Buy-Rite. Leroy, the liar,
sells her food, then tells lies to everyone about her; years later
no one remembers the lies. Wasn't Leroy counterfeit like all kings.

Marie isn't counterfeit: nor is where you are now, in this thicket
of polished ribbony ink spelling near-certainty. Okay, Marie is dead.
She inhabits the texture of everything, even manuscripts. An angel

flowers whitely before you. You've got to make a life, you can't die,

nothing dies. One lie, that she cooked lizards and ate them.
She got everything at the Buy-Rite; she didn't have money, did she?
Something must have come in the mail. Or he gave her old food.

I'm Watching

I'm watching the show on a rotten TV, catching the story
through red and blue specks—images double often, and
the sound's dubbed, they're made to speak a foreign language.
This is one of my favorite kinds of art. What's going on?

Eve Love is Marie's reprobate daughter, or is she? Is Leroy
vicious, even bad? Should I keep calling him by his real name?
Who am I?
        Momma didn't like the name Ruby—
it sounded cheap—though she liked a particular woman
with that name: I'm avoiding telling you some things about

really real people, realer than I am. Leroy told her Ruby'd
died, and Momma was shocked—I told you she was sick, he said;
but Momma hadn't known that she should believe him that time.

Me, I'm not very real. I've worked at that: I can't stand
the fiction of living. I'd just as soon be like Marie, my one
remaining hero. Real. She died out there at the dump
and wasn't anything like I'm saying. Once, a woman from town
gave her a ride and asked her if she was happy. She said she
was doing what she wanted to do. She wasn't crazy you see.

Eve is not Marie's daughter, though maybe someone is.
Is there Mercy? An image of Tara once arose from my chest
        to help me out . . .
But I'm not crazy, though sometimes women I dream about
imply that I am. I'm intact. Really intact. Are you?

Living on Brackish Water

This time the deity was an androgyne, with dark brown
skin, long hair, and literally flashing white eyes.
(I opened my eyes; I was scared; the figure vanished.)

Will you suffocate me with your strangeness, though I'm
miserable as I am?

I liked hell; could I possibly like mercy better?

They try to make mercy less scary than it is by calling it art.
You are the hallucinatory hornbill, eat me to pieces, with
your thick pigmented beak. You are a dried hornbill head,
I put you in my mouth and dance and shake the shit out of you.
Your feathers are crunchy. I am you with new shell eyes,
they have some painted bloodshot lines, but they look wiser.

The people are always pilgrims. This is the worst gutter medicine
I've ever taken. I hope it's working
All primitive types gamble away their very circuitry.
But I'm not going to give myself up to anyone but the death fish.

Oh your eyes are flashing again, you terrifying bugger. Maybe I'm going to
　　give it up to you.
You don't want me to do right; or climb the ladder to the money couple
You don't even have decipherable wishes.

Hell

Hell was dripping with the blood from the sores on my thighs—

The girl said let me tell you you are a monster. I refused to
put on her monster mask; I have my own culture. But she put the mask
in her eyes. Then I entered hell.

Your face is made of rotten wood and your eyeholes are gouged out;
you have sores on your thighs because you're ugly; you
will never look like poetry because they aren't healed. You're too old.

There's too much food in hell; a man's in charge of sharks for our food,
some of which are still alive. He says he'll poison those. I have to get out of
your hell; I suppose the sharks bit my thighs; I have nothing against them.

The problem with the girls: they're afraid of this. Though they cast me into it.
　　It's just hell. I give up
on being afraid and on sequential time. Everything's happening all around me,
not in a line. Anyone but me

Anyone but me gets to be the human. Well then I won't be. Join a different
company. Room of luminous visionary beings: why not?

Deep Red Eve

I approach the elementary school in a big serious cloud. The teacher
is sick; others are in beds; someone has to heal all the people in the room.
The healer and the sick teacher are the same. Eve Love. She gets up
and changes from old to young. Changing Woman takes me home in a pickup.

Where do you want to go home to? How does this trance *belong*?

You know all they ever did anywhere was just make it up.

I look through the eyeholes now . . . I was the mother of anyone
You use me to be born. But I don't use you, I can't use anyone.
Nothing has ever been of use, except the sounds between letters, where all
　　　the vibrations of being alive are kept.

Cruel Chicks

Marie remembers that people turn against her—several
times; girls. It was often girls. This might be a master narrative,
cruel chicks. She can't remember words for them anymore—
is a woman like me? I have this shawl of skin; they were jealous of everything,

while the guys were out killing people and eating them. See men's house
architecture, with the sharp teeth of the faces on the human totem column.

This is the room of the city in which witches were once examined.
The beautiful gems associated with witches—topaz and zircon—
are represented in the windows of the inquisition room, semi-precious stones.

I'm trying not to remember; the girls were like my dogs. They liked
suddenly to growl: you have the wrong mask you won't be loved.
You have the mask of talent—you will be used, but not loved;
we will talk about the light through the window of the gems—
the yellow is perverse, the white cutting: we can't live without it, so
we hate you. I hate you the girl says. You're not like my dogs I say,

you're constructed: glued-on hair and fangs and pulpy genitals.

Inside the Patent, an Aside

It was as if I had come back, every morning
like a ghost though I didn't speak the language
or the language of ghosts. To live here without being of it
or of anywhere I'd lived including the night.
Who was I to observe anything? I had no love.
I let stories, events, sights enter me, because I existed:
even tones of voice, in more than one tongue. No one
cared who I was. The quartier's up and coming. What
is that? What good is that?

There is something familiar about these lines as I
say them . . . They've been said before; I've lived before,
have I? You traitor to your senses, no I haven't—I haven't
        even lived yet.

The Secret

Nobody knows who one is. Therefore I sought you
to tell you who I was though I didn't know—I keep trying
to prove my connection to the soil I stand on. I can't do that,
yet speak to someone of "la ville de mon coeur"
for at that moment I am only the one speaking.

If reality in all its details were but aspects of a voice
it would not be Language, rather, one would be obligated
to define voice. As in the voice of the rose; the voice
of rue des Messageries. The voice of your continuity in the body of M.

The secret is telling me to write by rote—okay I'm doing that—
until it speaks. Somewhere along the line it started to. It knows my course
though I don't. It would tell me to speak in French if it cared, it
doesn't give a shit—That's it talking now.

I am more powerful than a president; I am a charmed and desperate
poet speaking to everyone.

Keno

Leroy drove to the casinos to play keno, boring keno.
It had cooled down to the 90s by the time he got there;
he needed to go somewhere and not lie. If he could just keep his
mind on the numbers; not talk to any strangers. Anyway it's no fun

to lie to a stranger—no consequences. Leroy had been lying so
much he couldn't think straight. He'd told one woman her son

smoked weed, every single day, by the river. He'd told a man he'd seen
his wife in her black and white dress at the Red Dog. It was all fibs.
Or was it, as soon as he said it it felt true. Leroy had dark hair

making a peninsular shape down on his forehead; wavy hair;
he wore glasses, though he'd never read a word in his life.

He told everyone Marie was some sort of witch or crazy person—
he meant she too was inventing the world, and they
were in competition. He let her bring her dogs into the store,

every day, and fill a gallon bottle with tap water. He
couldn't help it. He couldn't help helping her. She wore a dark
long skirt, a brown long-sleeved shirt, and a hat, so you
couldn't see how dirty she'd get. Or maybe so you just

couldn't see her—He told someone she was scarred on the front
of her body; that he'd seen the scars above her shirt, lacey and white.
No one believed it of course, but it was true.

Monoculture

The creepy god I am resides in an alcove. Gold crumbles from my
cheeks where I sit, within walls like neon green snakeskin
Scaley. Feel it—This is what a "self" is like

supposedly banished. Ignore me, or make your wheedling "self"-
pitying noises—as if to cauterize me so you can be sterile.

You, dreaming about crazies, fearful of becoming one. What if
your yellow, enraged aspect gets activated again,
screaming out the logic of anger in a world that's bizarre enough
to have invented it. The human crank, do you know him?

Leroy selected numbers as if decoding a message from hell.
Hell trying to tell him he belonged to it; another voice in a wig
you're forbidden to wear. The spectator in him saw the silky
hairs, magenta. Across the room a mandala turns. All of us together
inside this fibrous gooey structure, seeing to our fate. Making up
stories that seem to correspond to it.

Ruby

Ruby lay cushioned, dead. She got sick and died, like
everyone. Leroy had told everyone she had cancer, but
at first they didn't believe him. She was the nicest thing,

people said. Too nice for Leroy maybe; and then he was

abandoned to his lies. Ruby hadn't been a lie, had she?
What is a lie? I think it's whatever you say about a physical
thing, like yourself. Isn't it? Leroy wonders. A lie
might be the truth, is Leroy's philosophy. Ruby loved me.

He collapses out at the burial. Just too hot, he says.
Marie watches from a distance, past the dusty trees
that border the cemetery, separating it from the gullies.
She's paying her respects: Leroy always helps her, though
he lies about her like crazy; but almost everyone does.

I mean *everyone* lies about Marie. I'm lying about her right now,
in order to pay my respects. Marie, I first wrote about

you in 1969 before you died. I no longer have
a copy of that story, in which you were walking on the
railroad tracks, counting the ties. I've always thought
about you. And I can remember Ruby's dark-
haired, dark-eyed looks. Forgive me, both of you, please.
     Leroy too.

Cellulite

The pretty cell of your womb presents you with the light of Eve Love.
She shoots heroin of course. Everything turns blue
I'm afraid when it wears off I'll want to do it again,
not because I'll crave it but out of a stupid mental compulsion.
Do you want to destroy yourself. No I know I am love
but I have compulsions I serve. The stone shark mother
grins and rests upright on her cunt, unique female figure carved in limestone.
The scene remains suspended in cough-syrup blue; I can't come down.
I despair of explaining anything to you. Mute in bed
in the elementary school. Got so sick I couldn't walk, she
carried me home. They act like they know why we're alive, because
Hiya! I'm Eve Love! They come into the thrift store, burnt out
but ambulant. I'd never turn anyone away. What's money for?
It's for belonging, isn't that a crock. Eve's friends said that
I was crazy. Now she's a famous rock star, anyone with tits and a
scratchy voice. You don't believe me? She lives forever.

Tongue

Here is an image of Eve Love, carved in basalt, basalt face,
headdress, neck and shoulders, twelve inches high. The headdress
four coils, plus spherical attachments ringing top and bottom
the lower row fringelike just above her eyebrows. Over the ears
larger spheroid shapes lying atop conical folds. Why are there
hands on her shoulders. Epaulets. But her face
eyes slitlike, a depth of basalt staring back of the delineated
lids, upper fold epicanthic; a large nose with fat nostrils, and
open mouth, full lower lip: the basalt tongue behind it.

I walk along the edge of the purple park at midnight
accompanied by one of the cruel girls—oh why not?
I am the bird of basalt won't stop singing all the lyrics to
In the Still of the Night, which has transformed over time into
a spooky tragic song. Or will this dream of mine fade out of sight.
Like the moon growing dim . . . But the true Eve Love is singing it.

Cuticle

There are effigies of Eve Love all over the world. Marie makes her own
out of cardboard, more cardboard. She draws her and then cuts her out
curly hair blobs, swirly ears, big round eyes and a smile—Hiya
I'm Eve Love. Eve holds her hands clasped in front of her breasts
she has big round hips, a pubic slit, sturdy legs, and a lot of toes
with toenails. You rub a bit of your own cuticle on her and she
comes to life, according to the legends. Marie's just going to talk to her

as she is. The girls hate me but you don't. You're too weird. You've
always been weird: Eve Love laughs, I'm like you. Why are you on dope?
Marie asks. Everything's on dope, she says, the universe is chemicals—
you're on the dope of your setup out here. The dope of the girls' meanness

but you have a mushrooming regional economy in this dump!
They both cackle. You're gonna die of the sun, Eve Love says
Marie says well the whole world's going down in a blast of heat
isn't it? Eve picks up a broken cup and pours out a sip

of Leroy's water. I know you're not really here, Marie says,
it doesn't matter. She makes some mud and builds up Eve Love
from behind the cardboard facade. Oops, she puts some stuff
in the mud to make it stick together, shredded paper. I am

the mother of the territory; my demeanor is narrative—why can't I
help that? Oh little girl be hot and cold and think for yourself.
That's all I ask. I used to ask that you be happy, but
now I want you unbeholden to anyone in this far from credible cosmos.

Glossy Black Star

I got sick in the elementary grades at Vista Colorado; pains
in my knees and other joints so someone carried me home. I
didn't like my teacher, she was dumb, a smear of lipstick.
I had a spiritual malaise at that time, when I was seven; it's
unclear to me now. In the dream the teacher is another
and also myself, losing the grey in her hair to grow young
and become Eve Love. Who is a poet and knows my work.

The reason her friends think I might be nuts, in the dream,
is because I've walked over to the elementary school *in a dream*
but have awakened somewhere in transit. All in a cloud of un-
knowing. I don't know why I had my first malaise. Later
it's hard to find my house inside this huge all-encompassing
building that is the whole city of the world. The city of Mercy,
her body, even when it's ugly. No one needs any other gods,
for she emanates from within, and Eve shoots up to find her,
when she's a rock star. But I have no interest in naming
myself today. I am working at being peaceful inside
so the world can cease to be at war, and Mercy rest her arms.

Canticle

Marie resumes her French identity for an instant of pleasure in
fabric; a dress hemmed in lace (someone's dumped a skein of lace)
and a crown. Black and gold star stickers. Do you know that
        the Christ child is Eve Love?
A creepy greyskinned frère tells me that can be the case. I'm
surrounded by kachinas and ancestral spirits from everywhere
authorizing the acceptance of Marie as a similar spirit.
Marie declines, I'm my own god. Oh the kachinas say
we're just saying you can visit us if you want to. Or
you can call on us to protect you from the girls. A spirit
with a black hood head, with a central yellow stripe, is speaking.

It's raining like crazy in the land where Marie would wear frills.
A cathedral is Eve Love's doll house, isn't it Mom?
Are those two red flowers poppies? We are the poppies of the storm
Splat another drop on a fainting white rose. Our right eyes

are secretly enclosed in mystical triangles. We're all weirdos.
Everyone's in code, but you've deactivated the decipherment button.
I ate a piece of chocolate; it was turning to amber. Everything does.

Their Lipgloss

The girls rub shit on my house. They put on surgical gloves and rub their shit on the palm fronds, screaming childish curses, Mean cunt. If you differentiate yourself, are you calling out to the girls—if you do everything for yourself in no dress like theirs. As if your life was the wrong fabric and cut. It has to be like we say—girl stamps foot, classically.

I haven't bought into it, though I do sometimes spend whole days shaking. A form of payment: why must we pay for everything?

Shaking I offer you all my arms once again. In the urine-gold morning light, the amber light. Why don't you know how to talk to people? I talk to the dog-masks of the dogs. There is a flying fish on your face touching your long tongue: no it's just an effect of the urine-gold light. Your eye is mild in the swirls of your dog-mask, its gentle fibers: your eye is mild. Your mask is used to remove the taboo against two species connecting with each other.

The girls dream of me as their harmer, they enter a shack where I am, led on towards danger. The farther away from them I live, the more harmful I seem to be. It's possible they could try to kill me off, wearing their own ugly skulls, overmodeled with white pigment and uneasy lipgloss.

The Angel Squeals

Marie and her dogs have just left the Buy-Rite. Leroy
smiles at his inner vision: she will soon share 'loney
sandwiches with dogs—past-the-date boloney and bread.

There's a tree of malicious eyes somewhere in the world: each
branch holds a knowing, aggressive eye and the roots are a mouth
with pointed teeth: more teeth than a human's or dog's, a hundred.

Why am I so driven? It's as if I want to eat her or someone.

Compulsion, forbidden, penetrates Leroy's flesh and thought—
it could have been mercy could it. I will tell everyone Marie has
killed and eaten one of her dogs. No one knows how many she

has: why would she do that? It's a crazy rite to gain power
and endurance—dogs have stamina—and, they're almost
wolves. Coyotes. Any crazy person might eat a dog—
who knows what they think? Didn't she used to have a
pure white dog? No one's seen it in ages. She must have eaten it . . .

The white dog is a lie becoming fantasy—no one ever saw
it. Leroy will tell everyone she had it. Why. He sees it in a
quick dream: the dog had blue eyes and was clean. It
was probably her soul. She ate her soul. Why did she
do that? he wonders. Why did Marie eat her own soul?

Squint

I live in Paris, France, but I spend some time each year
in the Mohave Desert in the U.S. Improbable? This is the only
true thing I have to tell you. The only really true thing
There are no more borders in this world. You can watch your

computer like a TV. But fuck that. I couldn't stop being Marie—
or Eve Love—even in Paris. I couldn't stop being Mercy, or Leroy.

The king is entranced by his pain—sleeping through sentences
of grief decorated by the traditional deer, white, my love and the birds,
black with stark yellow beaks—No leader recalls his dreams.
Leroy pinned the ruby to his naked chest. I will never remember,

walking the streets of the city where Marie's scars are lace—
and mine are poems. The body mask made of bark cloth,
with tube eyes, another possibility. Long tubes to see through, bamboo
and long-fibered bark cloth speech pouring out of my mouth.
For there are no more borders. Ruby is dead but so many are
I get in a van with Hope, but he leaves, a sort of white-trash dirty
blond man who advises Don't duck: Eat the ducks.

At first the mike doesn't carry Eve Love's voice—it's faint;
but then, strong. I'm involved in a theatrical piece, she says—she
performs it too, kind of dirty. I have sex organs don't I? My
dad only likes Disneyland, not poetry, not this—I'll have to
confront him she says. Mercy doesn't care about dirty or not.

And I think I have to talk to her now—Past Hope, my
love oh words more than speech, than form or will or reflection,
I have need of you, the Mercy I know. The museum of the new spirit.

Retraction

You have become too large for your identity larger than the room
you sleep and awaken in, the details of it as mask recede, as you fail
to remember why you were worried, what age your face.
These loves too minuscule cannot pull you to mask earth,
a grounding in the demands of status and risk, passions of girls and kings

Then why does Mercy exist, if she doesn't care in particulars
if nothing one does moves her, vile or affectionate?

All she does is use her power, continuously to forgive. Why act then?
I found myself with so many arms I could do nothing but
touch whoever reached towards me. My hands did not hold
objects—as in some depictions—they didn't have time to hold things.
Could I ever become too large to touch you? But I'm
not aware of each touch. But one arm must be holding the pen,
Madame.
              I have spoken very little since I came to this new space
but I *think*. Each entity thinks in all its parts without knowing,
consciously, all its thoughts: for one has more dimensions than this
molecular world. Yet I am recording who I am. Am I yours
veritably? As if my arms, my touch drove you on
forgiving you so you could continue to be absolved of each
step you took, on the old street of blood histories, again and again.

The Dog I Knew

The white dog stands at every corner; you can't swallow it enough
I thought I'd only seen it at the Buy-Rite but there it was

on the corner of rue Laffitte and rue La Fayette, on that darker
intersection of rue Chabrol and rue d'Hauteville, anywhere around me.
Fix eyes and keep walking; eat the ducks; how many souls

can one person have? Dog; attention; ellipsis. The previous
dog, five years past, had been Cerberus, who had licked the walls
where I slept, a band of death saliva surrounded me. The dead
girl in the room grabbed him and pulled him down into her sleep.

Marie's dogs aren't symbols. And she didn't eat one—

Did you, though, swallow your soul. Can you keep it down.
Marie came into this world to master it in her own way
She changed your thoughts, because you had to see *her* some-
times, instead of the semi-naked girls with vinyl buttocks
imploring everyone to love them; I am building this culture out of will

and language and garbage. The dog spit sealing up the view
        is drying like glue.

The Codex

The codex from the dump is Marie's next priority, a true dump
manuscript, a book of pages of any paper, cardboard
covers, with text and illustrations in ink, crayon, the occasional blood,
and other pigments exactly at hand—char-black, rubbed leaf, there
        aren't often petals out here.

I will describe what comes to mind. I will draw it and
language it up: it will be *mine*, an enactment of my culture.
Does Marie know the word culture? I barely know it this morning—

it's important to use all the garbage, in the old way. Everything
we discard might be precious, though there's ever more of it,
and I intend to use it to make the being I'll become. Marie
will make a new world of one, out of our desperation, her talent. I am

my book: what else would I be? When I die I will be my book and
the spirit of creation, hovering over the desert, at midnight.

Tie

I thought to find you in the turquoise tissue paper crumpled
Tear out of the ancient dictionary the gemstones page or only
the heart-shaped bloodstone. It has veins. Remember? Write

Remember in black ink. I have cut out of my brain an image of a
lion that's petaled like a sun. Bright yellow, of course, but

it goes gold within the center of the wash, where pigment
draws together in a spasm. On the part of print, my mind

directs you into each ridged word I use, running through the
tinted interaction of your mind and the page. If I put Eve Love inside
she will pop out, fucked up or glowing with red mouth. I
know how to make whatever I want in my head; why do
I have to show it to you? Red paperclip. To match paint mouth
chalky rouge flaw.

Once Again

I walk into the body of grey Tara, the lotus cloud, encompassing
the elementary school and the desert and mountains behind. This is
a fully bloomed grey lotus. I don't have to know anything, any

more. Nonetheless there are words in the grain of the cloud

You are becoming the most elementary of beings. Help us. Why?
You can't bear to see us suffer. This is true, but why?
We are connected to the same lotus. I still don't see why I
have to. Be connected to the same lotus. Why did she have
to carry you home, that other time? Red wind flash on
page. I couldn't walk anymore inside the connection, with
dumbbells, who might also be vicious. Now? Now I don't care

Grey Tara touches everyone in the elementary school classroom
The dumb red lipstick smear teacher loses her ability to be
dumb; has tears in her eyes; she can't remember why she
became so stupid. She walks through the grey halls unknowing
her dumbness. What is there to do? Nothing. All the children
exiting the classrooms staring at the cloud enveloping
them. It's recess—We must not suffer when we grow up:
teacher, what is suffering? It lies outside this cloud.

There are a few silver and gold and purple sparkles in the cloud
You can touch a sparkle; it's gritty, confirming your sense of touch.

I am Mercy the word; you wrote me and I came to you touching
inside your brain and spinal cord. You can walk now, unafraid.

Popular Nature vs the Codex

A picture of a person may be better than a person, the girl thinks
The girl wants to be a person pictured; in your mind or on your
screen a stunning surface.

In Marie's Codex the girl is presented with crayon-drawn
round face and a pucker. Marie puts literal lipstick on the
mouth, geranium. Why isn't this girl Eve Love? She'd
like to be, but it's too scary: Eve Love has o.d.'d; and then written
a song of reconciliation with her soul: "I swallow you baby, over and
over / you're the one who cares, my glittering eternal self /
my soothing wilderness of righteousness / petal torn and gliding,
unexaggerated / I want you."

Poppeia's Hair

The more evil you are, the more convoluted your hairstyle? You
should do something with your locks, take off that hat
Marie considers gluing dead snakes to a helmet, can only
find one rattler. She skins it, dries out the stink, and finds some
other serpentine shapes: a piece of rope, a thick length of grosgrain,
part of a mop: What's this for? I don't know. It goes
with a mask painted black, with red zigzag lightning on one cheek
I'll wear it for some sort of rite. Rain and fertility? Naw . . .

naw, I will be Evil as Awe. Let's face it the cosmos is wicked, for
it kills us. So when I put this head on, I assume the universe's own
craving for violence. But I won't be violent, except as I dance
convulsively. I'll just *get it* . . .

I get it. It's *terrible*, a terrible power. I'm going to try to emanate
a counterforce. It's necessary to be more benign than life . . .

Marie writes the experience into the codex. Fatiguing, so
Mercy appears, floating in the mercy mask, with all its attached arms.
Mercy touches her and she sleeps; it's dusk; there are quail nearby,
in their family groups. To protect the spirit of feathers, to be in love.

Antithesis Police (Dark Blue)

Leroy's erased in his dream: red's covered over with blue.
She's gone—and so I'm gone. Who am I? Any old story will do
That's what they don't understand about lies. Not a pathology

Oh get up. Leroy arises; everything's in place. The Buy-Rite's
still there. Why do I doubt myself? Do I have a soul? What
does it do? It oversees me tenderly and cunningly, being Now.

Marie enters the Buy-Rite. Can't you leave the dogs outside?
There's nowhere to tie them; the stupid girls will tease them
Four dogs. What happened to your white dog, Marie? I don't
have a white dog. But Leroy knows she swallowed it, her soul
She ate it. She has hers. You swallow your soul so it won't fly
away, mine's flying from me, he thinks. Thinks down deep.
Did you eat your dog, Marie? Don't tease me, she says. Please.
She takes her stuff and leaves. Leroy's afraid he's had a sick
train of thought. What does it matter what I think? It doesn't matter
        at all.

Approaching Others

The girls stand in front of Marie looking like wooden figures
I can't mean that, not like wooden painted fierce-eyed
ritual spirits, with chicken feathers, resin and beeswax and rootlets
on their helmet heads, and huge ears shaped like butterflies. But I

want to see that, those, not the girls. Riding a soul canoe. Not like
the modern people product, She's looking at me! one screams;
her dog's gonna bite me shrieks another. They make a lot of noise
    and run away.
Marie wonders if she has to go to ritual hell with them again No

I have work to do on the codex. On my culture.

One of the things Marie does is straighten up the dump.
As she goes through stuff. She piles it up neatly. Some people
burn things out here—frequent small fires leaving black big
cindery flakes, beautiful. Everything discarded's interesting, a decision
HAS to be made, you say, ditch one-armed half-bald doll, and if you
    tried to conflagrate it,
Her rubber self doesn't burn well,

Good. For she was as real, practically, as one of the girls. They have
    dreadful little souls.

A Tale of Mercy

I told you she is I, though I myself call on her. So,
she isn't precisely an angel or goddess, am I? I have put

myself in the position of being an easy touch. Nothing else. I'd
touch anyone to give them relief. If I can. But my definition
is that I can. Who defined me? My culture, a culture of mercy,
a living codex. I am a unique culture of one, from everywhere.
I am her map and her self. I am everyone in the story; I
am the story. They say you can only see in space. It's possible
she is space. Or one is? Is there space? I'm the arms of it.

An angel has loose hands and feet—a definition—loose
extensions for healing, feeling, grasping. I saw the angel
in purple and blue. An intensification of grey. It doesn't
have to be one thing. Can my lineage or presence be explained?

Oh, around the 6th century the concept of Tara was elaborated
in the north of India, from where it passed to Java and Tibet. I'm
older than that—Poetry touches you with sounds on the back
of your neck. I touch myself and lose my social presentation of
clothes and hair, becoming crystalline, plasmatic, soul of the
crescent harp. She healed her own father, remember?
    Leroy the king sat in the dry wash crying

a nearby serpent will bite him. Call on white Tara
for snakebites; this is real, *oh real*. Was he trying unconsciously to
die? He won't die. Can you keep one of your hands on the wound till
the ambulance comes? He's lying by the athel trees near the river;
he was crying and careless; a stranger found him; he won't die.

Unplanted, I

The universe drifts inside a mind, like a seed that doesn't think where
to go. Snakebitten, I'm delirious; who will believe me if I survive?
Who believes anything but their own lies? or someone else's,
the universe drifts inside a brain, a tissue of lies, a structure in space
    formed by eyes,

before I first lied. What am I afraid of? Ruby died. That, and that
nothing will stay still—like in a *real* world. I'm hovering, turning
above the blue-green river, enraptured by my pain. *I always*
knew it, the worst would come—what kind of cosmos is that?
I didn't ask to be a liar; I didn't ask to be dignified or not; to realize
the truth or not; to be a decent man or not; to be meaningful to you—
    Who the hell are you?

Leroy's Brain

It's September in the codex—a gold ink month. Snakebite healing
he wears a sling, but no one believes he's been bitten. A fall,
a sprain . . . Marie believes him; she sees lots of snakes around . . .

But here's the funny thing. The shock of the bite—and the trauma
of Ruby's death—make Leroy tell the truth. Though it sounds
    more than ever like lies.

I talk to her, he says, I see her in heaven. He hasn't had this
experience, has he? What do you think? The brain
exists to soothe you, it tells you how to see the right thing.
The brain is the big trick: you tell it what your codex is. So you can

see that. I talk to her, he says, I see her in the afterlife. Sure you do.
And, if you can describe a vision, maybe that's having it too.
I talk to her, I see her in the afterlife. Fuck it, I do.

Eve Love's Prophecy

I stand in a capital of cobwebs, menaced
by shadows achieving meaning / enough to scratch at my contact
lenses and say, See us. Grieve, sister, they say. Get out of my
song, I'll grieve when I want. Right now

I just want to SEE, without brambles like you in front of me,
        stressing me out.

Oh city when nothing will exist, except burnt tendrils, massive
wires, sinews falling out of air. Your towers once grew like wildflowers
and now see after the guest hordes will have arrived
and be destroyed / by their own / fecklessness and violence.
        We will burn

ourselves up. I remember a friend found out in the desert
in lotus position, seared dead but upright. He still sings:

The future, emptied of consequences, has resonance. But I
can't explain that / I am that / calling back to you from
        our tribal silence.

Subsisting on Shades

The ancient injunction against sibilance reflects herpetophobia.
Marie cuts out four paper snakes and interweaves them,
two horizontals over and under two verticals, pasted, painted

isn't it a Mayan glyph? Naw I was playing around—
And pastes the whole into the codex—Now, it's in my brain.
        It's real
It's a meditation on Leroy's new condition. He doesn't lie.
Earnestness in his brown eyes behind the glasses

he's now a true-born serpent, he's himself; found his nature
does it unreflectingly. I saw her in the afterlife, he says.
I asked her, Are you happy? That's not how I think,
she says, You have the manner of one of the living.

Ruby's in his codex, Marie thinks. His invisible codex, his brain,
        his own.

He has the manner of one of the living; Ruby herself has
no codex is his meaning. I wonder what she has.

Sandpaper

How can there be a shark in the desert? There isn't but I
know about sharks. So they're in my culture. How can you
be in Paris? That's where I am, as I evolve my desert

Sandpaper use mental sandpaper on this maquette of a Paris
    infirmary.

He was in a hospital one of whose names is La Pitié, to have spinal
surgery. The other bed in the room occupied by a young
man injured in a car crash: a French kid whose ambition
had been, truly, to become a kickboxer: he'd walk now but couldn't ever
be an athlete. Full of self-pity and despair. His mother came to
sit with him, calm him, as I was showing a poem to my husband, who said
that he found it difficult. You have to hear it I said and read a passage—
in English of course. And then the other guy's mother said, Mais
ça, c'est très beau! She got it from its sound. Poetry is la pitié. Everyone
    was quiet.

Muslin

The girls come at dusk wearing red paint

on their lips and cheeks, shouting they are Satanists; one
has red paste jewels in her hair. Everyone's such a hack ritualist.
I the poet dream of the girls and wake up shaking in Paris.
They say they are driven by their fathers to be sexual
Satanists; they carry the AIDS virus. They say they have to

be like this. Does anyone have to do anything? You can just die . . .

I have to do what Daddy says. He makes me real.

Carp Shoals and Tules

Marie goes down to the river to fish for a carp. She has an old
mended net; she stands in the shallows and nets one, in a little
backwater from the big current, back here in the ugly shady trees.

Once she caught a chuckawalla with a sharp stick, rammed it
into its big airy torso. Flat fatty. She roasted it. Everything
tastes like chicken—rattlesnake does, cottontail does. Marie
doesn't own a gun. You can eat caterpillars and grasshoppers

Why not? But don't let the girls see you. Or anyone else.

She's thinking about a daughter, a house on fire—
she feels her scars—But she's not really thinking; she doesn't
have to think about it, does she? Not like in thinking,
you don't have to face everything. Every time someone burns
down her shack. It's like they know; but they don't.

Standing in the river cools off the scars. No one sees me
You don't have to get over it. You don't have to do anything.
I'm never going to get over it. I'm never going to think
about it. Oh standing in iced sapphires in this heat,
catching a fish. Haul it up in the net; and take it home.

Fill Out Questionnaire for Good

I couldn't find you in my metrics but I couldn't change it
could I? I couldn't change my language; I couldn't change

my father or his name. I couldn't rip the rubies out of my
hair; and when I went to her shack to scream whore at her

I knew I was that word. But there is no whore. My feelings
of discomfort are an argument for eternity—you don't
know what I mean? But you aren't here. I mean my feelings
may be transitory but are absolute in the moment, I have
stayed so long in moments, so deeply in them that
I came close to being god. Though I felt like someone who

had fallen from unconditional grace: it would love you
no matter what, but you might leave it out of curiosity—
isn't this way of being tiresome? If I went to hell would I

care, would it really be different from heaven? No
I don't know what I'm saying; these aren't my answers.
I don't care about being alive—women don't care about
that, they just care about you. Oh you. Only you.

Tidal Black

Ruby says, It's fussy here. And I can't find myself yet
I'm small and big, both, and I'm not comfortable with that
I don't even know what I look like. It's black here
I'm frightened as if I were going to die but I'm dead.

That's what she said, Leroy says. He's devastated. He's even
telling his stories to Marie. There's nothing there but squiggly

dreams she says; it's cold though she doesn't feel cold. It's like a
cold mind. He says. You can grow to like that, Marie says. Leroy

says, I don't know if you get to like things there. Are you
sure you're not talking to a part of yourself? Marie asks.
Oh what's the difference! he says. There aren't any differences
anywhere. I am her; I was her. This is what she tells me,

she's a small form that's become too large. Why does she have to be
the whole universe? And one small speck of it as well. She's having
  a nervous breakdown.

A New Way to Live a Life,

  This is what Marie has been working on. Not communitarily but singly.
Everyone doesn't have to be like her, no one's like anyone; and she doesn't want to
show them how to do it—how to be her—she doesn't know how.
  There's got to be another way to live a life . . .

Rabbit Skin

Write like an angel Marie writes, with a BIC pen, on a piece
of rabbit skin. *Write like an angel.* How do angels write?

I lost thee, I the stone head called Dawn, glyph shaped
like a double face—three eyes two noses two mouths.

Night's form a brown-black head, made of cubes,
a monumental Olmec sculpture. I mean, just some cubes.

Near Marie cigarettes spill out of a pack, twisted or squished;
some tobacco shreds leak out of them. A beautiful sight. Marie
stares, then paints it too. Is it a sign? What does it say?

Barking dog drifts along edge of dump hill. A pocket
mirror lies flashing signals to the left: everything's talking.

Violet Miss

Ruby wants to relax or, better, sleep with minimal dreaming:
I have things to meditate on in this rest, reasoning pictures.
Think. Dreams think. I am now used to the cold. I am a cold dreamer.

Crawling there you can catch train number one, slide through tunnel
        towards the track.
I won't go; it's too emotional, life, too demeaning to want to live.

Ride straight be a little girl on the track in manipulation's fist
Care for me oh my parent, with your firm hand; be my master plan:

Disgusting. Let go, Leroy, don't call me up. I must sleep until
        I know something.

Crapper Handle

Leroy has a vision while flushing the toilet: desert sun strikes
the crapper handle dazzling him. I tell you, she sleeps

in an extraterrestrial grave, an oblong volume of black air
nowhere, but everything's somewhere, and she can't unexist.
Not if she's in my brain floating like a spaceship, her eyes

shut, her mouth telling me things. Talking in her sleep:

They set the dead crow at maximum strength so it now, wow, flies—
all it ever wanted to do. I am blind in its gloss rushing. All
I ever wanted was a form of love, is this it, man? Maybe.

The strength of the feather in my hair. Stretching towards Antares.
The dead from all planets mingling tresses—or whatever they have.
We are loving each other to pieces . . . You never had to make it . . .
There are guys here who never even got to be born, didn't come close . . .

Tea Set

This is how I help people: I do nothing. I sit still in one of the
most well-known of thangkas. It's orange-red in this painting.
Once I was unhappy but now I don't move. What about the arms?
I don't always have them . . . It all comes from you; you have them

and heal yourself. As Green Tara I don't move; as Green Tara I
am red. I have the manner of one of the living; I must need help.

If all

your arms are at rest—I only have two in this aspect—perhaps you'd
like to sip tea from this exquisite Asian tea set. Thank you,

but I loathe tea. Tara, will you help me? Yes, all you need to do
is touch the back of your own neck. I do this and my outer
body dissolves . . . I become luminous Tara white. It feels like nothing.
The codex of my brain is working on itself; the thangkas paint themselves.

This Red Ink

I gave it to you from the brooding jar I bled into—
not a mirage, written in the unreassuring very liquid
of giving myself away. I did this. For you. There's a record

the codex is a library of tones and other intangibles
there are other colors of ink: purple, gold, turquoise—you've
already met them—amber, thyme, and jet. These
are some of the colors of my forbidden blood, spilled into

patterns down rue du Faubourg Poissonnière between
Avenue Bonne-Nouvelle and Avenue Autre-Nouvelle. I'm
always dizzy these days, but still a passenger advertising for a

future—haven't I leaked too much liquid to envision the
continuation of reason in the human written way, threadbare
landscape? Purchase a character, silly, and sit. Stop flowing,

I can't. I have to rewrite history from the vantage of one
alive a millennium from now, absolutely alone. That's

what it feels like; no polemics or opinions of the obsessing
vendors born to win. The signs collapse in the breeze
the bridges are gone and the conductors destroyed; the
colors are left, and the tones, to glue into a new outline,

into your lack, and there's an ecstasy in that. But how will I
be notorious? Oh I can live without respect, though
maybe not without dreams, at night, to cure me of the
dimensions. *Piling decades in a basket, just to throw away.*

Mercy's Teeth Defaced

I gave her a thousand arms and a shark's head—I wanted
her to have a dangerous smile. I put brown stains on
some of the teeth; otherwise they were just white spaces, who

can have that? But, Mercy is fucking wicked I tell you.
What are you going to do when you're let off the hook?
I like that: I paint a hook, one of her hands is a hook you
fall from into a vat of creamy sudsy compassion. There

you are swimming in it, with your happy curled mouth
and little X-eyes. Is it like that? The moon suddenly
appears in the Codex. He has a wicked face too, a vampire
grin and dirty-minded eyes with little lines beneath.
What are you going to do with your cleaned-up life,
get bored and be mean again? Marie never does, because

she isn't mean; when she's bored she observes boredom
brushing it onto the page with texture of fine-haired
indigo or ocher stroke. A shark tore me to pieces. Oh well.

Tara Talk

I'm trying to remember who I am: there's never time.
Maybe there isn't anything, though I'm here. The proposition

of original and ultimate nothingness is foolish, a human conceit. Am I
a human conceit? I don't have time to find out, helping you heal again.

I was in a line of women plugging in lightbulbs or devices,
electrical, one by one. I had to do some minute repairs on mine;
standing in line, the others go around me, it will be my
turn when I have fixed, or adjusted, or assembled, small filaments.

This is all I remember of my life, so far, this inadequate story.
Some say I'm a furious divinity with a third eye and hissing
hair: I don't believe in religion; I only do what I do.

They want their trees to be green—they're begging: I only do what
I do. I can't help nature, only you. Make some bongos and play
them, call nature back. I have extra hands, I can help you
beat the drum. Cover the bongos with bandages—they need to be
      healed too.

Point

Eve Love shows up singing: This shark says Stop Suffering
Just stop it, Daddy, she says. Stop feeling bad.

The ruse of inquietude keeps you jackoffs going. I suppose
you really are unquiet. Like the grave of power:
Stop haunting me—she sings—from the druidic hour
when you owned the symbols. I own them now. Protectress?

I'll protect you, if you'll give up your armies of malfeasance,
poor shits fighting for you—why should anyone
fight for a shoe that kicks its own watchdogs? This shark says

To suffer, especially for a leader or general, for a name of a
person other than a lover, is to be inconsolably dumb.

Like a criminal inquiry you want to know if I'm on drugs or
love whom I please. How did a dry corpse like you
get rousted from antiquity, from the pompous long-dead,
to harass me? Do the fucking dead fathers have

any fucking rights? You guilty heap of ashes
I'll soothe you with my song, if you'll listen to it.

Labels

Leroy says, Ruby says she'll be pissed off if she's reborn. She
doesn't believe in the wheel of life and no religion should have its way.

I'm beginning to believe in where I am, she says. We don't need
to know what we are, here. I'm forgetting, but I'm not frightened.

Don't think about me, she says. I saw her last night, and I wasn't asleep—

some of her teeth were black when she smiled. Her hair's tangled:
she doesn't care. You don't know if you're hearing me correctly,
she says . . . What if you're imagining something, someone else?

Used Broccoli

The diamond eye in my virginal forehead is bleeding,
millennia of supplies, it is a joy, not to see the tribe going to work
this morning: smeared red lens twinkling inward
away from the fine riddle of why they obey, they need supplies!
    which are everywhere

A guy whistles, "As we marched down to Fennario."

I remember wondering, when I was little, if I could stay alive
in the desert without anyone's help, without anyone or anything
around. There's always someone around—

The cruel girls have lampshades on their heads; hands holding up
castor beans for protection: *these are our poison weapons against you.*
They wave their beans at me and run away . . .

Integer grey, I don't react, I am merciful. Free in the desert of Indifferentistan.

Hello Multiple-Souled Individual in the Sand

Marie sits thinking about how many of her there are. Two, at least,
she says. Me, and me the Codex; but it's one, one soul me,

I paste it there. Deep green like socked in the chest. No one else can

do this to me—create me! I won't plug in that thrownout TV.
I dream better shows at night, lately in black and white: Burns
suspects Allen of murder . . . Or some WWII hero writes to Hitler,
I know who you are. That soul of my soul recedes on awakening . . .

Here is a new one I am. I remember a story: I lost her
in the fire, because Mercy couldn't put the fire out,
not even with a thousand arms. They burned us up, but I

ran. These scars tell my story, Dear, that you set the fire,
my human: you could do that. You were outside me, but
        neither one of my souls is.
Or is the Codex outside me somewhat? Who knows or cares?

Connect to Lens Mask

In Paris the desert is encrusted. With cement and acidulous history.
In 1313 le roi inaugurates the jewelbox chapel. I'm
sorry I've used any of these words but now I have. They're
imprinted on my once-bare codex page—in the glare of eyes.

Change. We're the mean girls. We will be fucked to pieces in the future,
we have gathered bird feathers to decorate our emotions. That is,
we've killed a hummingbird and pulled out its feathers. Fathers.

Change. I don't know how far back you can be something Asian . . .

Sorry but I seem to be everywhere, in every time. Purified, or raped—
resplendent with its bizarre vegetation the desert is everywhere,
        telling me what to say

The king will give us a beautiful place to pray. I will never
pray—he can't see inside me. I am now the desert.

Even if there's a gigantic flash flood. Even if my codex is swept away,
it is all my brain. And I'll have it. Even if the world is gone.

Wake, Out of Blue Crumbs

The casinos of finance—the Wheel of Fortune and the World—I draw
here as ring: the diamond-blaze ferris wheel at Concorde; or
a roulette wheel. The world economy controlled by gamblers:

Put on this ring and marry Chance as we name it. I'd rather paint
it and name it myself. O. Oh. Eyes- nose- and mouth-holes, a skull
with glutinous blue eyes, above a shirt. My old friend Loss,
the one who loses. I can make this mask as unfleshed as he's become—

what happened to your skin? I ask him, I mean ask the codex.
He's been drinking and grins. It's . . . he doesn't finish. I want to say,
burnt off. I can barely face him. He keeps grinning, in his skull-shaped
blood-vessel skin. Doesn't speak. A refugee from a fire. I'm hysterical,

No, it only happened in the codex. A story linked by jeweled colors
and letters. O. It is a dream . . .

Elementary Husk

Like harassing an iceberg with poppies. The ice has a pulp heart,
enraged. He the chosen vision. Don't want him, Eve Love says.
Everything has its boring attributes . . . Change them, shark with
your mindless eyes. Oh I will,

Screaming out from cunt mouth, because you think you KNOW,
until I grate the clock into my own philosopher screams—
Stick my mascara into his eye whites, flutter
insect lashes to excoriate the perceptual memos he'd say.
Living on borrowed responses. Well it keeps you in power, old man.

I'm still entering the elementary school. Come in, Eve Love.
If I can get past the fucking occluded teachers what I
need to know is somewhere maybe embedded in the grey walls—
rake em with my nails; scream and claw the swarming particles OUT

Where is something to KNOW?

They want you to go away; you won't learn what they say.

I want to know why my thighs are covered with scabs—
You wounded yourself deliberately. How could this world
LET ME, That's what I want TO KNOW! Emerald sobs.

Word Door

Walk through the word door, Marie. It's my own word,
a head with long ear-planks on top, tusks, and a nose from hair-
line to lipline, rectangular. I'm listening to you, the word says,
with my ear-planks. The word is red-ocher, black, and white.

I'm going to tell it stuff. The man set fire to my house, because
he wanted to. He didn't have an e-co-nom-ic motive; why
comes later, a traitor in words.

The word says under its long upthrust tusks, I'm a better
word than that. I have my own red eyes and rootlet hair . . .

He burnt up my baby and I just cut out. I didn't stay
to see justice done. Didn't care if it was. Justice is
a pretty bland word, says the word. It doesn't go at all,
Marie says. It seems to me I've been here ever since.

The word says, If the mean girls burn down your shack,
you need to keep me and the codex in a safe place. I've dug

a hole, Marie says to the word. Outside the shack,
away from it. I'm going to keep you in there, with a
piece of rusty metal on top. What word am I?
the word asks. You're the one I'm talking to now, you're

everything we've just said.

To Many

I've been flinching for years, Marie says to another word—
a bald naked figure crouching, with teeth and breasts and a navel:
lines of eyebrows in frown, of teeth clenched, fingertips to cheeks—
bones and vees of elbows and knees—it's a tense, brown word:

As if I were born to flinch. And others to make sure I do.
If you've been through a shock then you have. So leave it . . . but

the flames surrounded the crib and ate her. I back out
with my chest on fire, and turn; slowly; as my shanty—
my best house—goes up. The person who set it was nobody,
too, and he didn't matter. She didn't even cry, it was so quick. I walked

or sat, for days, in washes by the highway. I lost a lot of time.
Why did I go on? I have to make *you*, Word, but there isn't a reason.

You're fascinating, and you think. You let me look at you: we're related.
I'm going to give you a second navel beneath your heart.

Lapis Fumble

I can't get out, stuck in dark blue stone. I'm cold.
You could be stuck here with all your history
so far, not starting again. I went to school with
a pyromaniac, maybe he burned his way out of indigo.

Here come the girls to burn down Marie's shack again.
They just do it. They'll get away with it. The shack isn't *property*—
  no *permit*—

she doesn't *own it*. And she isn't inside. She's just
coming back from the Buy-Rite; sees the girls running away
into town. The Satanist girl wearing a red necklace.

The real Marie—that isn't what happened to the real Marie—

the real Marie was run over twice, in the 60s, by army
jeeps: the army had arrived for war games in the desert.
She wasn't supposed to be there, in the desert: I mean
they didn't expect to see her walking by the road, with her
dogs, so they *didn't* see her. They ran over her. Twice.
She got back up.

The Satanist girl is so real to me, that I know whose daughter
she might be. Because in town people all have something, even
if it's tragic. They live here because they're not ordinary
assholes defined by their outer trappings: they're defined by
their relation to the elements, and to the human elements
of cruelty, fate, and idiosyncrasy.

                    The stone I
am of is this desert—which underlies the planet—
threatening to take it back and catch us up in a geological
layer. Anytime, you know, you might rejoin Beauty.
Without a deed, a building permit, a necklace, a jeep. Without
a city or culture. I maintain a culture of one, because I can almost
control it. Marie will sleep outdoors tonight and build a new
shack tomorrow.

Summer

The mean girls run to the house of the Satanist girl
on the steep steep hill: the steepest hill in town: the front
way's straight up and barely paved, but there's a graduated back
way—up from gullies, and creosote bushes. The Satanist

girl, who's around fourteen, knows she's too old for these games;
but I don't want to leave fantasy to become some hack woman—
a house with credenzas, appliances, vaginal claptrap. I'd rather

have Guilt, for burning down her shack. Later. For now we're

Satanists, she tells the girls. Don't we need some boys for that?
the girls ask. They'll take us over, tell us what to do, she says.
There are a lot of things we can do without them. Call on
the devil, for example. He can be our boyfriend.

I Photograph Consequences

*I entered the elementary school and found Eve there. I seemed
to become her later, but she's too young for me to be.*

You can cut little pieces of skin from your thighs to make scars—
I, I haven't done this. I dreamed of these scabs but didn't
know how I'd gotten them. Life has its sub rosa hell, I'd say.
The students were enveloped in Mercy's cloud that day

because I entered the school to change its mandate. So
Eve Love could take me home. Girls would be fucked, but profound
consequence would wiggle clear to help you change, Red-

silk wearing women. I'm gazing at an echo in a tunnel

Eve Love, take me home. Even in Paris, where I don't belong
but have lived for fifteen years. I am brash enough
she says, to take you to the home you mean. It's always
in a fucking poem. Dog's direction. A poem that smells.
Always practically there but never am.

I thought I needed to escape the culture of rarified
slanted troped alphabetical philosophy, but what can
I escape? You can escape a corrupt old age, Eve
Love says. Come with me, poetry mother, to an inevitable
horizon, along the hot and grey path of the negative way.

The Future of T.

Mercy can sleep a little, moving her arms automatically.
Do I dream of what I can't remember, or of the future?
Unsaintly the air feels nearer: I'll endorse you for years,
it says. But is this what I'll be doing, after the abolition
of human nature? You partake of that, the air hums.
Human nature, oh do I. It seems to be about jealousy—
craving what others have—or a craving to destroy it,
anyone else's velvet. But, who's jealous of me? And

this isn't a dream. Though I'm almost asleep, touching the un-
kind, the bitter, the envious, with these hands . . .

I asked the kids to pack and run away with me. Sort
and pack their jeans of grey corduroy, so we could escape.
Always to run over ridges, or along cliffs towards
the sacred bunkbeds. Get out of these American conditions,

Leave this house; but it's not mine. What house can I
ever keep? My monogram M is in the bedroom.
A Frenchman stands near the fireplace: you've conquered
fire, have you? Where will I run to? No one goes with me—
I'm going to be captured, am I? They need a saint, don't they.
The horizon smoke of the alembic stretches too far:
someone should comfort them as it gets worse? That
tree needs more salt, that lily, cement dust. No I'm
leaving, no I'm caught: I hate these dreams, where I'm tacked up
in hell—your mind. I'd rather be awake, with arms. All along

the grey moment not night or day. We could have been free,
I always say, do I? Each hand writes a poem to your weakness.

You're just supposed to sing It's all right, the air sulks.
That's what Mercy is. Really completely healing.
Forget it, I see broken eggs everywhere; in the bedroom
with the ripped linoleum. Dreaming, I'll insert my
contact lenses—with which hand? I don't own a thing;
I sit. She's standing by a grave; someone's being looked for
in primary grades; demeaning sexual positions—well, are they?
I'm supposed to be Asian, far back as you can go. Well, isn't that
wonderful? I'd better start humming, or all the bad music
I absorb will take over my mental instrument, if you can call it

that. Remembering? Was I, Mercy, born in a hospital? I was
born in a brain. Like anything we know, the man says.
A brain made out of air. But not an airhead. Tell that
to the air! I must have been the first one there was. If it is
a mercy to exist. Well is it? It could be. So maybe I'm the basis—
am I? You're everything, a voice says. I want to cry. Who designed
your grey mist wool pants suit? a journalist asks. But this is a dream,

it isn't what I'm like. Sing the egg back into the shell. It can be
a different kind of egg. A scrambled chicken, or a film of its
burning punishment for trying to live. And when you arrived,
I could live? But I was the first one living! Before the epidemic
made me merciful. Before they said Stay, and starve—Tara always skinny.
Doing what you ask. Paved roadbed of your needs,
as they become the flat entity of the experience of me. How simple!
Your hummingbird urges lie dead on the slovenly gravel.
Of my admission of your case, stuck with feathers to my palm.
It's just osmosis. We're all still alive—and you will never be happy.
And I will always have this stupid job.

Tottering Un

There's a card game called Destitution, played with a Tarot deck,
in which you bet all you have—your house—against the house.
Don't draw the Falling Tower obviously. Marie got it again: But I wasn't
        playing the game!

Leroy says to Marie. You've gotta be part of how WE
do things. (Ruby's whispering in Leroy's ear: No one owns anything . . .)

Marie says, I guess I've been playing Destitution for years—
well why not? Everybody gambles, Leroy says. I'm playing
it again, she says. I've put up more boards and palm fronds.
Playing games against the girls? he asks. It's always against the house,

the rules makers—their shitty little fathers, Marie says and walks out
of the Buy-Rite, angry at the light. You're blind, she says
into the light. At home—yes it's home—she paints a new
Tarot card, the Dead Tower. It can't be struck and toppled because

it's dead. Two black-window dead eyes. The top half
is gone; the lower half's an ivory skull. It's dead. It's just
      a fucking dead old house.

Scars

A sear tulip of white worm trashes my body. Stars
scream, however else you name it. No real animal knows this,
so unapologetic. See these other funny chest lilies, my brood.
But they love you. How do you want to talk now, in the new

way of living? I don't know if I have a choice. Even if I
      sound different.

I move deliberately. Bringing palm fronds from the date ranch.

Precious mind, at the bottom of the grotto, interior
pool place. Time breathes, returning to my cell.
The Satanist girl has been spying on me by herself.
A virgin already tired of sex; it's the approved destiny . . . sex

strangling you with obsolescence. They progress as far as
the cog, the present participle, the first word on the wall. *Mean.*

Tear down factory girl and boy with the weather.
They may have to say good-bye before they find out what
the new way of living is. Nerve telling you to do. What next.

Someone Put You Out

We destroyed Marie's house. How mean have we become? Outside
the window of the house of the Satanist girl, see the black
doberman pulling on his leash. His name is Satan.
I mean it; I mean there was a dog named Satan. Why

in such a small and isolated town did someone have a killer dog?
My daddy loves that dog. A mean dog isn't intrinsically
mean, some say, he's trained. I mean someone trained him
to be more meaningful than a mutt. Or the two white dogs

Marie puts into a collage in the codex: though she
doesn't yet know what they mean. I think we'd better

call on the Devil now; we're doomed, the girls say.

Do you know how to? they ask the red-necklaced Satanist.
I think we have to walk out to the cemetery—take
a short cut over the clayey path, through the long
gully, straight to the athel trees and the graveyard, avoiding

the highway. You have to lie down on a grave. But we know
all of these families. Do it anyway. Lie down on Mrs. Chavez,
she wouldn't care. But it's supposed to be creepy! I'll
do it, the Satanist says. I'll lie down on the grave of . . . this one,

where you can't read the name anymore. The weather's rubbed it out.
Died ages ago. Doesn't mean a thing.

Visualization

She stares straight up at the dusk sky without blinking. It's
like a cataleptic trance. Finally one of the other girls shouts,
Talk to us. What do you see? Do you see him? I see
a circular face, a moon with a lippy smile, not

anyone in particular. Not even a guy. It's talking . . . Her voice
        deepens, Sweetheart
there's nothing. In the sense of ectoplasmic—what's that?
        a girl asks—
certainty. There ain't no devil. She laughs . . . No god
either. You're it! Science? It's a baby. I hate your

big tongue, the Satanist girl says in her own voice. Moon-
face says, I can't help it, and it isn't there. If you believe in
something you'll get ahead, dear; if you want something.
        You have to want

the previous pattern of wallpaper . . . Cheerio! She sits up
and tears start. It's as horrible as I suspected. Everything

we're expected to become is a hoax. But I want
a boyfriend and stuff! a mean girl says. I want love! Don't

you? I don't want anything . . . She thinks, I'm like Marie
and shudders. The girls see her body shake and they scream, You saw
the Devil. That face was the Devil! You did it! You talked to him!

Ready Birds

Eve Love and the Urchins play soon in the Desert Theater.
People will sleep on bedrolls, up and down Broadway,

waiting. Should she change the band's name to the Sharks?
Her own teeth are growing again—she's ready; do you under-
stand the Concept / I am not only an image: I can kill
you with Love / the dangerous cancellation / of your

store-bought soiled nation / with its sickly striped bass to eat /
swimming in the oil-stained flooded street / the undignified
the funerary tide / of your wooden capabilities, empty
destructors / brainless figures, I am for you: Have I come

to help you desist? I am the essence of your times, its very
kiss. We are on our way out, though I can never die
never leave you. I will never be less than what you cultivated—

abandoned village replete with liminal site. Walk through
the theater door—that building's been closed for twenty years.

Ivory Ivy

The carved ivy's entangled in the form of a slab: does
this mental image serve a purpose? Marie feels she must
honor it. What is it for? How render it . . . She draws the ivy,

then streaks on house paint from a not-quite empty tossed
can and writes "ivory ivy" alongside. Soon she remembers
the kicker: I had previously slept with the man who killed
my baby. Because it was possible; anyone might, you know

anyone might sleep with anyone. He was lonely, but
the attention bewildered him: he had eland eyes, other-
wise awkward of body. She supposes he burned her house
because she was kind—won't remember his name. He had

to see flames: he followed his impulse—satisfied his desire,
     didn't he? Marie is speaking

to the image—it's too painful to be a letter, with a letter's
swirling whisper. It stands for death—not her child's in the fire,
the arsonist's soul-death from wishing, a strand of the tangle
of empty impulses. This world. The World is the ultimate card!

You don't know what to do with it. I'm entangled with him.

Portion

This is my portion. Mercy—Tara—says. It's what's
in my hands, always being given back. The celebration

of me by my devotees is in fact a plea for ease—heartsease—
I'm murmuring again, rhyming like a fiend. Please,

they say, please. Sometimes pansy; sometimes wallflower;
sometimes a cognitive disease, the doubleback blues. Blue Tara
crosses the seas of your bad decisions to comfort you: But why
should you have had to decide? The night is coarse,

my knees are hoarse from kneeling in front of an
emaciated female. No, *I'm* Tara. Anorexic; don't
have time to eat the haphazard peas they leave on the
altar. You're just too grouchy. I called to her with

my orchestra of consonantal bees and desert vowels,
accumulated unpaid fees to the whining fates;
you owe us more sound! But I don't owe Tara a thing.

I have the keys to the house and the pickup, my mother said.
Then she was driving the pickup backwards downhill, while
calling on a cellphone to see if we had assurance. We don't; she's
laughing. Don't worry! But I take over the wheel. I hate

these plays, verisimilitudinous, enacted near casinos, with men
as top cheese—they lose for us, admonish us, predict recuperation
of small change from the lees licensed to clay effigies, you,
me. Oh Tara! I only want to feel blissful for a second . . . !

I can't feel like that, she says, but maybe you can.

A Science of Ghosts

Who are the ghosts? Are they thoughts; are they letters of the alphabet;
memories; emotions; or the dead? Leroy used to be a liar—
were his lies ghosts? Is Ruby, the ghost, an hallucination,
an imagination? It doesn't matter, not to me, Leroy thinks.

He's unpacking cans. I've always hated stewed tomatoes . . . thinks . . .
That thought is a ghost. King of red mush, geometric shapes'
information, unpacked from a trucked-in box. Ghost.
Clank. Clank blam. I don't care if this Ruby's real or not: I don't

know how else to get through time at this point. Another
fucker who does what he does. That's all I am. But

I'm not lying! No, Leroy isn't lying. The king of lies
has ceased to lie. Can Ruby, gone, leave him? What will he
have if she does?

                Why do you always
write about talking to the dead? People talk to the dead,
that's why. And history, knowledge, every formal discipline,
all procedures for being alive are haunts! Ever in contact with ghosts,

you walk between two white dogs, two, simply two,
for each side of you, your escort. They are beautiful, clean,
and dead. Down rue du Faubourg Poissonnière once more.

The Girls Mature

One of the girls has had sex. I slept with that guy at the gas
station on the east end of town, where the trucks go. He's
almost twenty, he's too old for you. We're Satanists, we can
do what we want. I didn't like it very much: it hurt.
I mean I liked it, I like him, but it hurt. But maybe

it always hurts for Satanists. Did he look weird? We
weren't very naked—in the car. Is sex right for us? I think so.
Better than hanging around graves. The Satanist

red-necklace leader thinks, the group is about to break up. I
know it. How do I know these things? Last night I dreamed
streaks of gold paint made me say things. It wasn't
light, it was paint. It wasn't religion either. A streak
of gold would throb and I would say words. Everyone's
shucking us, scamming us. Everyone's dumb, at the same time.
Mean. Do I have to be cruel to grow up?

End Lock

Some pennies someone tried to burn (it's against the law);
a cotton-filled pear, also apple, "dutch" yellow and red with green
undertones; harsh blue-star-splashed wrapping paper;
a rotten lace-edge hanky; one dangly rhinestone earring; a pen
nib; a page of sheet music from "Malagueña"; a torn
blouse, red, short-sleeved with white piping on collar and pocket:

leave it for the eyes. Of crows and lizards. Marie picks up

a mirror and looks in it: she's brown, and lined. I'm
beautiful, like a new face. I never had this one before—she's
barely looked at herself for years. There's no discomfiture
in my eyes; she smiles—Just who is this then? There
are the mountains, back there. They call themselves undecimated.
There's an abandoned refrigerator, too, in the mirror. This is no end.

II

Identity of a Mist

This codex is about identity. I can't help it.
What do you really think you have to do? Tara's

identity is so fixed she has no sense of self. Or beauty,

but I hear the buzzing and humming of letters, she says.
Different, over and over, where the vines trip up
false magicians. I cannot be debunked; grey as the edges
     of creepy awards.

I'm still trying to remember where the heartlessness of
care came from. I engulf the elementary school
in a cloud, so the children can finally branch out. Not
be set towards a terminus of skittering chances, dry
gale—you're supposed to be bored and superstitious. If you're

self-destructive, I say that's better. Though you shouldn't
die. I'd teach them to respect the gutter and the gully.

The old fathers have to enter the story at some point;
owning all the diamonds, still; coughing them up for
the cruel girls. What're you gonna do with your
jewel? Smear it with snatch juice and love it to death;
see if I care. It's a special kind of life, there in civilization.
But on the outer fringes you can probably lose your contempt.

The Second Time

The girl who's had sex says, We did it again. What
was it like this time? It didn't hurt; it was fine. We drove
out into the desert and did it in the car . . . That

was one second time, I'm speaking now. There's the second
time you watch a person die; is there a second breath? It's
too fast to count. The second civilization to collapse,
in relation to who, counting. Marie's last shack was her

second structure at the dump. Now I'm in the third
shack culture. This word means "ancient"
but it's better: I paint eyes, nose, and mouth on black
without a face. It's the next demon; the first one
was before ancient, the second one *is* ancient. When

do I get a face? the demon says. Who am I really? he

asks. Who called me into being? with lizard flicking
sounds. So I have ears. Marie says, You are the ancient

purveyor of unsteadiness. You hum future dissolution
from the corners of your bug eyes. Or do you
guard me? Maybe you guard me.

You Aren't Abstract

Marie relives the night spent in the hard arms of the firelover
I slept with his blank heart, truthless, of murder. It contorts me to go
near events; he was a divided object that fled my ground:
he was an objective word, with no sound in me. He was untrue.
He thought to like love, but didn't; because it bestows—I'm not
having these thoughts of him; foundered with his eyes, wouldn't see.
Refused. Would you wish him healed in his hard difference?
Would you kill him, want him transformed, or forgive him?
Blameful I let someone into mine including my child: I,
was I wrong? What use words? In the codex they've more thickness.
You see them, in your mind hear vibrations that the flat culture won't
grant a meaning; it isn't what's said till now in my whis-
pers only I am here, hurt by mind, rent from the world, and the world.

Tangled Jade

Ruby appears to Leroy with only one frontal eye
and a maw; she is sketched in gold against black,
finely delineated against all of black space. Terrifying.
Why the one eye? he manages to ask. Past, present,

future all at once, she says. Can you prophesy? he asks her—
Maybe, though the view's mixed up, or rather too true. The way

you see it, all parsed out, is kind of stupid. Oh why

do you have to be a *goddess* now? Leroy's sulking.
The goddess already existed, she says. I'm just—not filling

in, exactly, but sampling her. I'm nothing, really. I
can be anything. The gold threads tremble against

the black universal throat. She's awesome and ugly. Not his
Ruby anymore.

The Book of Lies

Do you believe this stuff or is it a story?
I believe every fucking word, but it is a story.

Don't swear so much. Aren't we decorous? What
        is a culture?
It's an enormous detailed lie lived in, wrought beliefs,
a loving fabrication. What's good about it? Nothing.
It keeps you going, but it institutionalizes inequality, killing,
and forced worship of questionable deities; it always presumes

an absolute: if no other an absolute of intelligence and insight.
The lore of certain people—men—what you're referred to.

This is Marie, thinking, though she wouldn't use this language;
this is also Eve Love thinking, though she's young enough
to bang her head against the wall thinking it: Marie would rather
reinvent the world for herself. This is Leroy thinking, who knows
more about lies than anyone. This isn't Mercy, or Ruby, or

the Satanist girl, or the girls, or their fathers thinking.
The Satanist girl almost thinks this; but she can't love
skepticism. It would make her cry. I, I don't think.
Except as a device. I think thought is a device. To get there.

Stop Pop

Can you remember him at all? I guess attractive, balding
and pale. He stepped out on his wife. He loved his killer dog.
Try to get the daughter's voice, wistful over him, but hardened—

I have to love him. Why does *he* have the right to leave when he
wants to? He could leave for ever; he *knows* he must act responsibly . . .

I think that's what I won't be like. Can't I not have it? No,
you have to keep caring about the ones you were placed in life
with. By no one; no power. That's what I know from being
a Satanist. There's no Satan or god, there's only this miasma

I am of, connected to people with claws and implosions,
people who defend their right to suffer inside the confines
of one private self with a moat. My father's a cheat, and I
        don't care why.
Motivation's no good: it feeds the doberman. Or clogs
your pores; we will cure you of your mystery. Oh will you?

No one I know *is* mysterious. Taking up too much space.
There he goes, not waving, off to the Couple Up.

My Eve

She's trying to decide what to wear for her concert
at the Desert Theater. This a nightmare in which
she's never ready on time. It doesn't matter what I wear—
      yes it does.

But you're wondering, is she really here? I mean in
      this town.
Her family lived there for a year, when she was ten—she
went—yes—to the elementary school. She had encounters

with Marie; then left, they moved to LA. She showed
musical talent, a suicidal rebelliousness; told her father
he was a greedy skeletal demon—he sells cars. She
makes gobs of money: her mother says she's a hypocrite.

I'll wear this tight black jacket with its clump of
artificial cherries, over a cream lace camisole, some
tight black silk pants with toreador ankle slits,
and high heels from the thrift store—scuffed chartreuse
      slingbacks.
I won't comb my hair, I'll look great. No one here,

no one coming, means anything to anyone in the world
of stars and breakdowns, contracts . . . No reporters,
it's truly nowhere. Why are you doing this? my agent asked.
I didn't know the answer.

The Kicker

I have to GET IT better, Marie says, so the codex knows more
and I can read that. It has to TELL ME better, so I have to make it
do that. How. Ways that I think most automatically. The dogs

of culture, for we have invented dogs. My father, said a woman
in my dream—as she played the piano impeccably, in the surf
along the coast—what is this about my father dying, with his
little dog there? The music the woman plays is beautiful,

note by note—I've never heard it before. How am I
hearing it, asleep like that? How write it down? Marie

draws her leaning over the piano, waves beat rocks, she has
long hair. Then Marie simplifies the drawing on another
page: profile hair arms, curve of piano, rock, splash:

I can't think too many things at once, the woman had said;
though maybe she can hear them in the music. The woman in the
drawing asks Marie, Am I a *word*? No, you're a state of mind,

one might call it thick understanding, but that's ugly.
You are The Woman Playing the Piano in the Ocean, Thinking of
her Father's Death near his Dog. Too complicated. You are sounds
    between words:

You Are: *I only wanted to find you again; instead I found beauty.*

The Fathers

The fathers are imbibing at the Red Dog and the Sundowner.
The Satanist girl's father is on his own at the Couple Up

wondering if he'll visit his girlfriend later—his secret
gigolette in the new riverfront houses—Desert Mansions—
when Leroy walks in. Gene doesn't want to talk to him—he'll
lie or tell a half-truth about Gene's being out on the loose;

looking to assert his dna, I mean HaHa. I mean Science
seems to tell a guy to go to it—dominate, spermificate
        (not a word—he's slightly drunk) . . .

Leroy's pale. Your daughter helped burn down Marie's
shack, he says. Who cares about Marie? says Gene. She's
garbage at the dump; her shack was garbage and needed
burning down. Marie's better than you are, Leroy says.

You fucking her? Gene asks. Ruby whispers in Leroy's ear, He's
a jerk in a terrestrial scenario. He's a planetary local, earthling
stereotype. Let's get out of here, Leroy; I'm about

to say good-bye. You should treat your daughter better,
Leroy says to Gene and walks out of the Couple Up.
Gene can't believe it: that certainly wasn't a lie. But he

doesn't care. I'm free, free to just sit here, he thinks.
A self-important lush, Ruby says. People will believe anything
that allows them to drool on their underwear. Or on
whatever's already there, some dollars, some mush.

Ruby Goes to Pieces

I can't translate myself into language any more.
She's one-eyed again but she's only the eye and a mouth.
I can't talk to you any more. The eyeball rolls up in its
socket—exertion of speaking: mouth trembles.

You're going to be all right, you don't lie now. I
know, Leroy says, but I don't understand why I don't;
and I'm not sure what good it is not to lie.
It, existentially, just, is, better! Ruby gets out. If, he says,

the World is a lie . . . Isn't, she says, if you're truthful.
Where is it? he asks. Oh, behind. Underneath. For the last time

she giggles. Then dissolves into a magenta hue against
midnight; thinning out; she's gone. Leroy's empty. Who am I?

He walks to his car. Should I go up the river and gamble?
Should I let myself into the store and work late, unloading cans?

What Do You Wear?

I wear a magic invisible shark's outfit, grey but
invisible. That's one day, another day I'm wearing tits
and a penis, a feather on my head, and some smaller people
on my shoulders. One day I'm wearing the flaking mask
of the Phoenix Immortal, because I rush ahead of you
protecting you and showing the way. Another day I'm wearing a
wailing pigeon's voice—So what? So what? I was standing

in line for a haircut—why bother. The haircut lady
came outside to fix us up. I don't want to do this
any more, look a certain way for you . . . even jeans!
The woman from New Ireland has worn the same little
loincloth all her life. We're going to put you in jail if
you take off all your clothes: it's too cold, you jackoff, I won't.

A Brittle Treason

The girl who has now had sex betrays the Satanist girl—
she wants to try out betrayal and it's easy. First, she claims
she knows more than her because she has fucked and the Satanist hasn't—
the Satanist could claim that she's fucked Satan but she won't;

she's truthful, and the other knows this. The latter says to her,
I don't want to know you: you're too strange. And I don't like
the way your father looks at me. Says the Satanist, My father
doesn't bother to look at you: your ass is lame, and you don't have
boobs. The Satanist girl walks away. She hears the Moon-Face

calling: This is a sorry culture, babe. You have to make your own.

Desert Doorbell

I rang the doorbell of nothing there. Air on dirt,
mountains scary and close enough. Gold lit nothing. I
rang it. I wasn't selling anything; I wanted stuff.
I wanted to know what dreaming is; I wanted not

to suffer; I wanted energy, happiness, and peace. Exactly that

out in the middle of nowhere. A dream, a dream had told me, is

an illuminated word. Okay but why? Oh I don't know,
I'm just the dream. Nothing knows nothing. Mercy touched me

when I was suffering once—how? She doesn't know. Well who
fucking knows? You can't not suffer though; you can't have
energy, happiness, and peace. Well why not? Only the rich
and powerful get those. The Buddha said otherwise. That liar.

I rang the doorbell again. You can't get anything in this
style. Yeah, I can. Mercy floated towards me, towards
the door not there and opened it with one of those hands. If I
can just remember, she said: maybe I can remember
my own story for myself. Even if I don't have one. Remember, for myself.

I Questioned Your Lovable Pill

I stood in the fire, as if that were the only place I'd ever been. Then
it changed to mist, the lotus petals cooling me—you're
spared. You can be loved ... Is that what I'm supposed to want?

Some father stuck you in the fire . . . some king or general.
Dole out mercy to poor shits who serve his likenesses. Nothing
ever changes; no one gets smarter; I can't remember who
I am—You're so repetitive. When I engulf the elementary school

with my mercy, *I'm* inside. You musn't burn, I say to her . . .

if I could just stop suffering in the past. This is the sick
joke of the doctrine of reincarnation; reborn moment by moment
to never die, or change, reborn as your Tara, and her constituents—
the doctrine keeps us all down: the spiritual generals sing

the praises of their words, their vaunted reasoning
process: I can't even REMEMBER! Stop repeating that.

The man takes me to a house in the country, another man's inside,
purporting to be daily life: my oldest friend, he says greeting
me. I'd trust daily life, if I could trust these two but I can't.
I've got to get on a plane. Before those woods are on fire again . . .

You didn't have the right to make me Tara!

The king tried to destroy her and she forgave him, over and over. NO!
I'm screaming, NO! but my arms keep reaching.

Sock Him

Eve Love, backstage, contemplates her razor blade: there
isn't time to slice at her thighs, is there? She puts it away . . .

Outside the theater's dark—oh it's been dark for thirty years—
this town is commercially a ghost town: all the small
businesses changed into a Wal-Mart; for flicks it's casino movie houses,
just across the state line. The Desert Theater has been cleaned up

but it's shabby. The old plush carpet still in place, the art-deco
light fixtures on the wall, the red curtain, the geometrically
patterned ceiling, dark-beamed hexagons against yellow cream.
Eve rehearsed in the afternoon with the Sharks, and you could

hear it all over town . . . Someone enters her makeshift
dressing room: an asshole preacher who cries out, Jezebel
and other archaic tripe. Eve, who is six feet tall, socks him, yeah
she makes a fist and punches his left eye.

Is She Stupid

Marie cannot believe how beautiful—and she made it—
this codex page inscribed with nothing she'd imagined
before: it's an accident. In the midst of poster paint purple,
a certain tremulous hand, like hers, skinny-fingered
but you know it's touching you because it does. Feel it—

just some mammalian paw, that's pulled itself through time's
ooze? No, no evolutionary theory admits of mercy or the trans-
mission of such through oculatory stimulation, or tone of voice:

Marie hears the hand humming. She has made it,
and it is saving her. Glorify it some more. She has a book
of flower stickers: pansies, forget-me-nots, red roses, carnations,

and she pastes some around the edges. Adds gilt paint glints
to the purple, soft roar of the hand of assuagement—

Marie has created the icon of peace and rest by herself.
She is in beauty, falls asleep dreaming of a dove's murmur.

Marble Eyes

Should I swallow the lovely drug? now or after pro-
crastination. Which flower should one take. Tincture of
hallucination, wild energy or heavenly drowsiness . . . Altering

the syntax of narration, its pace and vocabularic exigencies.
      The man

is behaving badly, having been allowed to paw one for fifty
      thousand years.
He has orgasms on his résumés: I am the master
of penchants for survival lust melting on the horsehair
blanket. In the office or at war. String of images; cleaning

the paintings on walls of a cave; there's a swallow failing,
acid holes in its wings. I've taken too much of the drug. I
sing shudderingly well, endangered for the art. Mister

vacant shards with no face and marble eyes, why are you
watching me like that? The ones you see clearly when
you're high: he's dangerous, Mercy he's got a gun!
No it's his deformed stem hand, with blunt tendrils
clapping against those other ones, fragments of stapled skin.

Don't Bawl

I stopped caring what you wanted me to say; I stopped
caring what you wanted me to do. I pulled back my
hands but kept singing. Couldn't stop. What else would
you have me do? Is my name Mercy or Maso-

chist? You'd call me either wouldn't you. I pulled back
my hands and stopped. The night without Mercy you called it.

Do it for yourself, I said. I'm gonna remember or die.
I'm sitting in the dark with my thousand arms folded.
Humming. Singing. Eve Love's performing my song, on
the drug, designer wormwood; doesn't know why
these words pass into and out of her. The Sharks keep up.

When did I start being nice. You're not loving me
back. Change your shitty diaper, outside the church and grow up;
I reject the theology I'm in, but I can't stop, can't stop,
howling in the night without mercy, married to my
species. How can I get out. A goddess can't die; I zoom

like a witch skittering over troublesome mountains.
These are the hills of hell, my love: no love. No one
loved Mercy back; that was the point. I never asked

for this. Have you gone crazy? Mercy has always been
loved. I remember the first time I walked. Then
you made me sit down. For forever.

Daddy Masked Me

Leroy sits in the Desert Theater, listening to Eve Love sing—
Where's Marie? She's outside; she wouldn't go in;
sitting in the alley behind the theater with her dogs,
hears everything. Something merciless is happening:

Eve Love is singing without love. She's screaming with lost
hate—drowning in emotion, can't find its sides for pity's
sake. It won't let her out. Can't you go there on automatic?
To pathos or Love Me or even Kiss My Feet, You Sucker—

an inversion, but love's invitation still? No, it's all the
planets have gone out; the blood from my razored
thighs streams in the unreconciliating skies: My nerves
are everywhere exploding with uncomplicated grief:

Can't get out, can't get out. Can't remember

any other tone. Her voice hates itself: have you ever
heard this, sister, the rain beats my ass with centuries
of lurching, badly executed stick-figure tangos,
behind my scorched eyelids, comparsitas yap and reel too fast—

Marie's fascinated by this hateful music. Leroy's crying
like Ruby's leaving him again. But it's Mercy who has left
for one night; you're alone, can't you take it? I've got to think.
Unplugged. Languages of despair are dispersed through

the atmosphere, in terrible colors; my powerful daughter's
    unmasked.

The Ancestors Return Raving

Every fucking dreaming night they come back, dead as formaldehyded
sharks, dead as bark canoes, as penised and bump-hipped deities,
and dead as everyone I ever knew. Accept the past—
but I'm so sick of it!—and get together with the deceased

in black dust apartments; remember the O.D.'d. They alive
perusing lush green posters of the transiently famous, with you: *Post*
columnists no one else recalls, B actors in RKO westerns:
I remember when you was a girl with a nickname. Oh, wonderful . . .

Walk out into the pollution-index-seven air and buy the Sunday
papers. Who are you, a woman, what's that? Still

haven't made up minds what minds. Wind-socked
the minds fill while it's still light with capitalist blood-bite
frenzy, tags and confetti dotted. The sexist scrolls continue
to unroll in synchrony to the food, shelter, and energy rat bar: press
it, the ancestors shout; I had a great idea, but now I'm

too old etcetera. And anyway I'm totally alone. I
went one stop to the Gare de l'Est, bought the Observer On Sunday,
and Le Journal du Dimanche. My horoscope says give everyone
        air kisses this week.

Bighorn

The Satanist girl, listening to Eve, starts to block it with
her own thought. An indigenous voice converses with her,

inside, no one; someone faceless to talk to. Have you
ever seen a bighorn sheep? I've been to the Dead Mountains,
where you might see one. I didn't. My father drove us there,
when the springs were full, and violet flowers bloomed.

But I walked all the way to the Dead Mountains in a dream,
wearing a pink sack dress and white, low-heeled shoes. It
was sick black night. Why did you go there? Who knows?
I've been in the Dead Mountains all day awake lately.
Here, they're here. I'm afraid I'm already dead. Everyone

walks an aboriginal trail, but rock art's obscure to the
stupidos. *I* know what it says: BORN DEAD.

Ancient art is replete with examples of eternal beauty!

It all spells death to me. And this singer's dead too.

The Codex Eats Me

The dogs tell me it could be worse: I could be eaten by
oversubtlety rather than bold red or blue letters howling,

HOWLING! That word again. The dogs open their mouths
    to word me.
Have you ever dreamed you didn't have a master. We dreamed
we ran down the gully to the river, but not without you; we
couldn't leave you. I entered this desert long past the middle

of my life, knowing that I could only have what I wanted
on paper. Everything's covered with dog hairs; shake them
off the illuminated pages, no they're painted on, ocher, gold,
and black filaments. I stepped outside the city of Paris,
and there was sun on water in clear air—surely a dream.
The past loved you, though it didn't know you, but

it projected itself towards my melancholy. Have I betrayed
        the past?
Electricity and laughter, taunting, are inscribed on this page.
The old house full of creepy scholars, walking all over
colorful decades, squashing them with large, ignorant feet.
Can't you paint over their faces? Here is another

D for dog—a dog undermines anyone, whether it's the
dog of death, or the dog of dreams: more oscillating
hairs, white, shaded with grey and purple; or thinly gilded.
D persecutes you with its sweet disposition. Yet I dreamed
that a mean man announced, in veiled irritation—for
the dog had been part of his power—*The dog is dead. A new
dog will arise. Who volunteers to take charge of it?*
A healer raised her hand; but so did others. Who will be assigned

to this office? Who can call Death to order, now that the planet
has lost its blessing? No one.

Marie's Underwear

Can I stay with you tonight? Leroy asks Marie. He's left
the concert early, but the music's all over town: "We will
never be alive again," sings Eve Love, "Never be the species we
once were. You won't recover from this loss, my lovers;

　　you won't be there . . ."

I can't stand it, Leroy says, I can't be alone.

(And where has Mercy gone, on this haunted pearline night,
incandescent with fear—there's a lime-colored light all
around the rim of the sky . . . She still sits with her arms
folded, high over the elementary school, too high to be seen,

high enough to remember . . . ?) Leroy and Marie enter Marie's

shack. At first they sit, he bleak, she more like curious: what's
happening? We should make love, she says. And takes
off her shirt and skirt. Her underwear's white and clean;
her scars are livid. Leroy begins to kiss them: what else can he do?

Swimming in Sacred Water

The dogs have run away from Eve's singing; they've gone
down to the river and are paddling with the current close to
the shore. The water appeases their fear of her voice:
is water sacred because it's only itself? Like them; like I

am, a dog almost thinks. Her coat darkens to chocolate
with yellow glints, her wolfish snout smiles, red-tongued.
Beloved water, you are the only cure when sunflowers stretch

across my eyes, hot as veracity. The song blunts, but if
the dogs knew words they could make them out:
the glaciers of passion are melting, my love / and there won't be
a thing but your heat, for thousands of years. My heat
joins yours, where we'll be together, no longer
living, my love. And Mercy says, Look what you've done:
Why should I help you forget it? I'm tired of forgetting

everything. I want my details: why shouldn't I have them?
I want not to have been on the margin, pretending to be good.

Obsidian Necklace

They said it was all about sex; but it was all about power. Have
you ever noticed that Mercy doesn't have any? A man
climbs stairs, a woman sits below, looking rich but
waiting: if you start up they push you back down, because
you're not as hard as obsidian; your true memories

have never hardened, only the approved, societal ones.

Why I remember. No you don't. I was a child. Oh were you?
I believe I've always been the same, M says. Nothing
happened inside me except for shock—then I knew the
universe was false, false to me like a traitor—is that

its character. Is treason the meaning of life? You're supposed
to yearn for a lover. I wanted one at one time, but I don't
remember anymore. It doesn't seem like the truth; I

got myself into this predicament of offering assistance,
by buying what some guy said: We're depending on you. And
he was. He wanted me to cover his ass; he would continue
to fill the high positions, fuck up, repent, and hold on. I
would make y'all feel better, especially women; I am your

final role model, girls. I remember all this. Particulars? None.
There aren't any particulars now. No one knows
a goddamned thing. So how can you suppose you remember? I
remember you: I touched you, you dumb blur.

This necklace is very hard and I'm putting it on. It stands
for what I'll never know. It stands for the despair I've
dispersed through Eve Love tonight. And for what you do to me.

Think of it this way, a new saying, It's only Mercy's hate.

Satan Barks Again

Satan the doberman, leashed, won't stop barking . . .
The Satanist girl has left Eve Love's endless concert

and gone home. Eve's songs can be heard faintly, "Who
loves each other, in the evasive dawn, when the cuckoo
sings no more? . . ." The Satanist girl wants to
stroke her father's dog, but he isn't lovable, is he.

Do I have a future. I think it's called discomfort. My
Satanist sisters are too dumb to see the black athels
blocking traditional contentment. My guts are burning ...

I've never been a child or a girl. Why should I be?
I never use my name to myself—why should I?
I didn't name me. I wear red because I like the color.
I need to see it to feel sane ... Eve Love should shut up now;
Can't we make her stop ... ? My Dad's drunk and not even
listening; my Mom's got the TV on: applause of the eradication of brains.

Far from Thought

There are adventures recorded in my scars; they're there
not in mind. So, what you see is my past unrewarded,
     Marie says.

And, I can tell you all the lies I've told ... No, I can't
remember them. Everything that happened. No,
most of what happens is a lie. There is no record
but lies: why can't I lie? I'm not really here, am I?
     Leroy says.

You're kissing my scars, my mind, Marie says. My mind

hurts a little.

Eve Love is getting tired onstage; the Sharks can barely play;
it's almost dawn. Fatigue is a good, she sings. It makes me

stop crying. Makes me stop being your baby. Makes
    my mind leave.

Diamond

No one is qualified to criticize me, the mourning dove calls.
Are birds sexist sexist sexist, like people people people, the cactus wren cries.
There's nowhere to live in this junkheap town, laments the burrowing owl.
I have no money, friends, or hope. Says the air to its damaged self.

He disapproved of me in my dream. Then I awoke; it's
too warm for février. Observe your thoughts: are they a poem? No.
A long time ago something happened, that I embody.
These clumsy, untrue words, given to me by my ancestors
will insure my election to the presidency of a country of self-deceiving fools.

The words say, We are not untrue; we are words. Try us
again. There is a pure codex in your heart of Marie, glittering.
I can't draw or paint very well, or even glue things neatly.
The real codex is invisible; I'll continue to work on the false
one. Plato sat down beside her dogs, with a tin cup of camp coffee.
Her lover had gone, I guess. Marie's lover, Leroy, had left.

I awaken in Paris and drink a small cup of Carte Noire.

Blue Dot Between Eyes

I haven't dreamed for days; the membrane's closed over, of the blue
dot: my other sense. No one can help me now. To do what.

Inside Mercy her loneliness reclusters and at some future date
it will harden into a frilled chalcedony formation. It used
to be diffuse, but now it is an ancient kiss. She is worse, much

worse. Elsewhere, obligatory the boring party with spiked lemonade—
it looks yellow, metallic. People standing around the morning
after the concert pretending that it was terrific. Eve
has passed out in her motel room. The Sharks are so
freaked they can't move; drinking and shaking as the desert sun

rises, hot, taking the sky like a battleship.

I don't know as anyone in town slept last night,
the Satanist girl's mother says, in their house on the steep
steep hill. The Satanist girl thinks, No one can help me now.

Lie Junk

When I used to lie, people feared me; for the lies were half-true:
your son's on big-time drugs—in fact it was only once—
I think he got a syringe from a diabetic: who sat with him while he
shot up, in the bushes with those dusty small pink flowers

out in the wash behind the hospital, did it there . . . Leroy feels
guilty for every lie; he starts to remember them all: That her

husband put his hand on that silly waitress's ass—it was her arm;
that his daughter stole my wife's birth control pills; that

he was drunk as hell himself, I saw him stumbling at noon—
keep a nip in the office, do you? I saw Mrs. Gutierrez
come on to her neighbor, that fat-butt sluggard: put her face
one inch from his, he just stared at her. She isn't very pretty,

not like her daughter in her too-tight tank top, fuchsia
torpedo boobs. Leroy thinks, I could never stop . . .
Partly I wanted to stir them up. I wanted to see them have
feelings—But I wanted the power. I never made them
better, in my stories, than they were: only worse . . . Now

I've slept with Marie, and it seems like a lie. My snakebite:
venom cures venom? For there was that too, I hated
them: Why? Because we were all too dumb. No, that's not

right. I want to be able to make the world—I hate this
one. But I can't; and I can't be nice, and I don't want to be.
If I am, just *am* nice, then, that's another matter.

Evil Nymphs

I can never vote for a man again, but the cruel girls will.

The cruel girls are skinny-dipping in the river,
plotting to burn down Marie's shack once more;
the Satanist girl isn't there. They've gone way up river
where no one can see them. One girl says,

What's the point, we've burned it down before? The girl
who's had sex says, bossily, That's the point: to get
rid of her trash, to keep her out of our world. Okay.
They all say, unconvinced. They have swimsuit tans on their
unimpressive bodies, just humans; they don't even look

alike, like iguanas, or pallid bats, or pack rats—perfect
animals. The girls don't really know why they're naked,
they're embarrassed; hurry into clothes. Let's go get a coke.

The Bar Code of My Lover's Kiss

Eve Love approaches Marie. The latter sits before her shack,
painting with a brush missing part of its bristles, on dis-
colored scrap paper—horizontal lines. Is that a bar code,
Marie? Sure! I figure every lover needs one: I

don't know if it's mine or his. They both laugh, the way
they always do. Eve Love looks terrible, her shirt isn't
        all the way buttoned,
hair uncombed for two days. The concert really beat you
up, didn't it? Eve sits down in the dirt too.

It was exhausting. It was like channeling half the
cemeteries on the planet: Some species force freaked out . . .

You haven't been cutting yourself? Too tired.

Marie hands her a stick of spearmint gum. You sleeping
with someone? Eve asks Marie. Would I tell? But isn't sex all
that counts? Eve Love jokes. Maybe no one's really

a person, Marie says. What are we? Spirits, motion. The
first and only thing there is. Sex's bar code won't stay still.
Marie messes up the bar code with a hurricane of
        squiggle. It looks a lot better.

Coming Up on the Famous Hoax

A lot of animals spend time alone—polar bears, orangutans.
Breaking your solitude is as painful. As being stabbed
or burned? Too melodramatic, says Marie,
watching Eve Love leave. You say I should want to

be with; you who are someone inside me, pretending to be
the Authority. The Authority is an ancestral remnant, a
memory of a chieftain's hat made of straw, roots, flowers,
and monkey dung, chewed up vitamins, hair, seedpearls

and epoxy: Big Magic. *I am the One Who Knows.* I
am always banishing you, but you keep returning
in your Hoax Hat. There's nothing anyone says that I have

to accept; there's no one else here, well the dogs; and lizards
etc. But Eve and Leroy could kill me, simply by existing.
They're in front of me, not inside me, breaking my
heart: I keep letting them, out of curiosity. I don't

want love. I want it to be called something else. Or
nothing at all.

Iron Stairs

The past was never better; it's built in. To remember a thing
you have to analyze yourself. Why do you never age, Mercy—
I haven't had time, I mean, I've had all the time in the world:
one little instant.

I was navigating the West Side around 13th Street, on a
wheeled platform, like legless beggars used to use. I couldn't
stand up—"You're all arms." Then I did, falteringly, and
you said I'd once healed someone, your friend. This is a book
I wrote, The Dreams of a Beggar. This is my box of a hundred amulets,
a thousand poems with dazzling powers, one for each arm. Now
you have to climb the male stairs. Why can't I dynamite the staircase?

Hello Jeannie, and Eileen, my delicate cousins. You won't
enter the poetry reading. It's too conceited tonight;
it's boring and unskilled. I mean, the Mercy deliverance—Every-
one's standing outside the room not listening. I'll tell you
my poem out here on the porch in the dry warm Western
air. Do you hear it? That's *my* touch. I love you in
your paleness and sheath dresses. But you're not the real poet,

someone says. The real one's that dead blond guy, singing
and playing the guitar, in the dark Roman amphitheater. You,
you have to take care of us. Still. No; I am the woman with
a hundred visages and frowns. A thousand trains of thought . . .

I remember when he shut me up in old stones. The tale
bores you, but you're still in the rock, my ladies; etched and stressed
in sexual posturings. Can't I be merciful to the girls modeling
their underwear? someone asks. They have to do everything
practically nude. It's genetic, says a white-coated shape-shifter.
Everything's the way it's meant to be; I'm the meaning, he says.

How do I blow up the staircase? With TNT for each arm?
It's the best kind of iron in the world: they built these stairs out of
certitude. It's a spiral, darling, ascending to some presidency,
the position called the one who matters most. I remember
when it was made, out of a clever tone of voice, and memos left in all
regions—he dreamed me, he thought, and I was dreaming him as dreamer.
But, too, I was dreaming something else, because his dream's
intolerable. I dream the iron staircase crumbles; the he's fall off it
shattering. Do I touch their broken bones? The staircase fragments
form a new brothel. An old man shows his yellow teeth: yes,
back in the old place. Then, I'm refusing to be dreamed by you any longer . . .

I rig mechanical arms to a generator and walk away. You'll
never know the difference, I say. I'm going to disestablish time
and sing away your mirage.

Embracing the Shark

I don't know if you can filet a shark or not . . . You'd shrink
it first. I'm shrinking the shark but not fileting it . . .
Marie discusses the subject with the letter as she paints it:

You're shaped like a fish, and you stand for embracing the shark.
I am probably a glyph, the letter says to her, sanctimoniously.

You are a damned shrunk shark. The woman who is also shrunk
is riding in your mouth, legs inside, torso out, and she looks ahead
at the water. You don't eat her legs. Why not? Because
you're embracing back, and that's how you do it. There's a funny-

looking bird standing on your head. I want to eat your legs,
the letter says. You're a letter not a shark, and it isn't me. Why do I want
to hug you? The act of hug is *within* you, as the concept depicted.
You don't talk like that, says the letter. I know I don't: that's why I
paint letters, glyphs, things no one's ever read before . . .

You can't make words with us, us letters, the letter says.
You aren't syste*matic*, Marie says carefully. I don't want
to close this world in. This codex. A fortune-teller
told me I'd never be satisfied by any country, any culture,

any *program* in this world. On this planet. I'm not;
and I don't intend to be. She says. Applying more red ocher.

The Geode's Promise

The purple crystals inside me are owned by me. The geode
rolled away before it could be split open, went downhill
and disappeared into its own diary. My promise is extinct.

Do I owe anyone anything? Marie asks. I showed Leroy my
scars, and now, in a way, he has them: I haven't escaped. But

I haven't told him about my baby. Don't think, she says
to herself. The image she's painting says to her, They always

get you though: you might as well think, to protect yourself.
What more can be done to me? she says. Plenty, it says—
she's painting the letter R in the bathtub: it's being cleansed.

I'm very clean, says R. Why am I the only one you washed?
I'm not telling myself why, Marie says. Is it because

I'm the first letter of the name of the man who burned
you and your baby? I wish that I could never think again,
Marie says. And now, and now I'm not thinking. She

paints a bird in the sky above the bathtub, which sits
in the desert in front of the Old Woman Mountains. The
R leans back in the tub, relaxing in the suds.

Paris Doll

Brightness, then it darkens in the snow and coughs. February
whispers, you fit well in my monotonous hand. Don't even

be a person, a character, a flash of prerogative and intent:
one espresso. Weather isn't pagan any more, not
here. There's supposed to be a flood sometime; we breathe nano-

particles of our sooty disinterest. If you've made everything
that's killing you, all of us, why we must have been in love
with death! Do you love death, I say to a mind; it

replies, It's where I was before: I wanted to feel at home.
My mind says, I disagree, you've never been dead, except
now; you're just a mood, composed of sulky clocks. I am
a noble culture, the mind says. Three hundred years of violin lessons,
hit by a meteorite one day while she was breathing. Beautiful

breath. She resembles gravitas, because of the label on her
upcoming grave: Played checkers with the (snicker) Matador.
That was when we still had epitaphs. I don't mean a thing;

and it is raining, in the ambulance called city.

You Wingèd

You grey harm, you insect letters, you unasperged and
aggressive; you populations of integers seeking ploy;
you crumbs, you people, you un-animals, you voters; you

bad weather. I didn't want to live among the millions
of secret agents, a person says, spies for the government
of the mimics of living, hierarchy of male men like a father/
feather brain leaking suspect consolations: hope, and cosmic
acquittal—isn't she a natural too? Is change a hairdo, you get a cut

then some disappointing foreplay. You get word. I get words,
Marie says; but you get the drift, a claw on the nape of your neck: Be

my Valentine. The cruel chicks think they're thinking again:
She's undemocratic, let's beat her up real bad. Lying awake

at 4 AM, there will be no substantial advance in stigmata
removal before you die, though the tattoos in the Codex will
never come off; but the girls' faces shine, thinking He's mine,
the latest mouth running for office to run you. Marie

is practicing new camouflage techniques in the gully of
escape. Avoid the authorities. But the girls
are in our hair, even are our hair. They have so much of it.
Love ya, America.

Primal Duration

One of Marie's dogs is half-coyote. Her bushy tail is black-
tipped; her muzzle is pointed and she stares, the way
coyotes look at you an instant before disappearing.
And she howls; yes, a song dog. People know she's half

wild. So the girls have decided not to burn Marie's
shack: too repetitious. They've decided to kill this dog,
because "she's wild." Marie calls the dog Tawny. The girls
want to feed Tawny glass: they bring a can of dog food

and an empty Dos Equis bottle, waiting for Tawny to
run off alone, as she does. They hide where the gully twists
away from the dump and towards the mountains:
they know Tawny comes here alone to hunt for rabbits.
This is her route, one says. They open the can of dog food,
break the bottle, and mix the glass in carefully with a fork,

leaving the food in the shade of a creosote so it won't
spoil before Tawny comes. She comes here every day,
around this time, the girl says.

The Doll Breaks

Tawny drags herself back to Marie, blood dripping
from her mouth. I must help this child die. Marie
holds her: a streak of red, brushed by Tawny's
tongue against the open codex page: the symbol for

my baby. Marie had drawn a face like her own,
but rounder; *my* baby—her eyes are circles,
blood on one cheek now. Tawny whimpers,
Marie strokes her, the other dogs watch. The sky

darkens inside my eyes: don't let me think or
act; or I will be violent. This has to be a moment of love.
I can't see. As Tawny dies, Mercy envelops them,
helplessly: I couldn't leave you. The darkness

is now grey and moist like a tear. Mercy touches them all—
I have gone wandering, but I always hear a call.

Peridots of Kings

There is no culture anywhere, in these countries I almost
live in; though there is history. And there was once—but
now only monolithic companies. I drove through
town—nothing left—a two-story ragged portion of the
Desert Theater; another building almost torn away, leaving
a structure with scant paint, couple of windows. Our
culture. I don't want to live in one of those in the
past future perfect tense. It isn't that I don't want to live.

In the south of France, Rousseau, the contemporary poet,
will now read. He sits at a table, facing a black window
that reflects him. I stand behind and stare at his image
intently: he is so plain. A woman staples her poems together—
then he cries out in a note. What a musical genius. We are so
fortunate to have him, whom no one cares about. I don't,

I'm my own poet. You don't need a poet; you don't need
anything but a big store. You don't even need yourselves. And
that's fine. I guess there wasn't anyone to write to. I
did it for the universe of ghosts; half coyote, half motel.

Eve Love Hooked

Eve's gone back to LA and gotten hooked on methamphetamine—
only temporarily, to get off all the other drugs: I wish
I was her right now. She's beautiful, revved and cheery,

her lipstick's on a little crooked, but she's writing genius
songs. I always feel so much better on speed / Walking
faster than corruption, blood unclotted. Who has a need /
to be a girl scattering pollen, programmed, on a biological

lead? . . . No one can do anything about her, thank
heavens—not for this unflawed vagrant moment.

You are the pearl in the distance you always sought;
wearing yourself in the hollow of your neck, a cloudless
sky. You don't have to feel for you; you don't cry, you,
the one you love, loves, transparent to the world of
folk lining the street like hyacinths in April. I want
to stay in the afterlife, but I'm getting a rasp in my
brain: I'm gonna come down.

Pieces of Mercy Flood the Downtown

Mercy cannot bear the death of Tawny: she's on her own,
floats wherever having left a machine in her place—the
Tara jackpot is what it's like: pull an arm and get a coin—
well wasn't money what you wanted? Oh, this is all

a *metaphor*! But compassion *is* something to keep you
going—dirty currency, go back to work: no one really
wants to change the world. You're, still, always waiting
    for Later!

Mercy despised her job: But the agony of a half-coyote
dog with glass in her guts hurts like hell. There's no

reprieve: and we won't celebrate Easter for you, a mutt,
a female mutt. Mercy's arms go crazy touching

everything in the vicinity, the dump and the gully,
the cemetery, and the downtown, near the railroad station.
She descends in cloud tatters onto Front Street, where
I first saw her in a dream, a year ago, retreating into
the old drugstore out of fear. I was afraid of her touch.

Now it's all I want—cover us with grey relief: we,
the denizens of the elementary school, the primal horde.

Rendezvous with a Final Fish

The death fish comes for Tawny. The soul canoe,
the shark: death eats you as you eat rabbits, my
dear. The canoe carries her and eats her, encrusted
with shells and pigment. No, she is an animal
        in the desert—

the desert boat comes for you, a lightweight river
canoe; no, the coyote spirit comes for her. The great

coyote shaman. Marie watches her own mind's imagery
settle on a coyote, with darker coat than normal,
coming closer and closer to them. Then taking a pup-
sized figment of Tawny away between her jaws. Tawny

expires. Marie's lap is filled with blood.

The Epic of the Guilty Mesh

It's years before I'll be able to gamble at the casinos. I
can kill a wild dog, and I can fuck, the cruel girl babbles,
Already; but I can't vote and I can't bet cash . . .
The cruel girl says, the one who's had sex. The other

girls are awed by Tawny's death—crouching behind
tall bushes. One is crying; Marie knows they're there.
She removes Tawny's head from her lap and walks
towards them: You're murderers. The crying

girl wails louder. I have no feeling for you; I'm
supposed to hate you, but you don't even exist.
You aren't even animals. Everyone in town knows you're
dirty! shouts the girl who's had sex. I'm not a murderer,
Marie says. And I don't burn down other people's
houses. But saying these things is so banal, she thinks
without thinking the word "banal." People are awful:

my mother thought they were good, but she was wrong.
Marie will bury Tawny herself, with a dump-found
broken shovel. This is so banal. They could be
warriors, or serial killers, or vengeful rejected courtesans.
They could be anyone who votes for a commander in chief
of the armed forces. Marie turns and says, You're

just anyone, and that's the worst thing I can say. I'm
being so banal, she thinks, without thinking the word.
Because, people hurt you and make you confront them—
so banal.

Diary

When I awoke I thought of the word Benediction, for
I have blessed other humans, in one respect by living,
consenting. We the alive consent to the procedure. Do I
consent to the casino, the ultimate result of our experiment?
But you don't even handle the shitty, dirty money yourself:
progress doesn't have the flavor of actual finger-smeared

devalued bills. It's tasteless and odorless. My check
on its way from Alabama. In the Plotinal high-level brokerage
the Real Money's manipulated by the Demiurge: but
the guy above him, Deity, never even touches the stuff,
though He grants us currency, so the myth of corruption

can be played out: What else would He do? He, she, or it. Do
        you get it? Marie
earns no money, doesn't use it; that's why the girls really hate
her. I, I try to get it when I can, without doing anything, except
        maybe writing this. The casinos

are redemptive, if you like to be bored. Redemption *is*
boring, isn't it? Streaming payback out of the pink
and orange slot-mouths; you're paid for having lived. I think
like this, I eat muesli for breakfast, I write poetry that will be

obliterated, or not, depending almost entirely on the actions
of others, who aren't sensible, want money, roar ahead.

Rich People's Codicils

I have a will and I have a supplementary will, the king said.
I will that Guanyin continue to *care*. I will your *obedience*
to my *notions*. A rope ladder of continuing stipulation—the self-
same one racks down from what I want. I want you to *get it*—
I mean your compassion is my compassion: I am meditating *you*
into a continuous existence: I am causing you, I am

causing your grace to imprison your reason, while you touch
with pity every lamentable situation I have caused
for my own good. I mean *your* good. *I'm* not confused.

Leroy's sick of unpacking cans of tomatoes and creamed corn.
Was I only someone when I lied, but that was no one.
Shrouded in the clamor of silence. Marie enters the store,
blood-spattered: The girls killed my dog. She collapses

onto an unopened carton of cans. What can we do? he
says. Nothing, she's already dead. I keep staying alive, he
says, in case what it's like changes. Blind options,

no one says, depending on the choices of five billion
people, who mostly don't know each other. I buried her,
Marie says. More momentum tomorrow; now a Greek dusk.

Leroy's Nightmare

I was riding in an elevator—there are no elevators in this desert
town—but I was riding up in a roomy one, chatting in a positive

tone with some people in the corner, when *she* entered. I saw
her again, and she would have been the beauty she had been—her

shoulder-length dark hair: what was she doing in a motor-
cycle jacket? With a fur collar. Maybe that's an aviator's? For

going up. But she only had one brown eye. And she said,
I'm sad I'm gonna see Leroy die. She didn't mean I

would die now. She meant my name would die, and there
would be only I. This doesn't make me so sad; for more
and more I am less I, Leroy, and more I, I. I can't explain
it, but that's how there's no liar left. I'm

in a house, in another landscape, flat with trees,
alone with you. It's almost night. Who are you?
You can't have a name either; they say your name's
Dick. Well you're gonna lose the word, and the

significance, and the act. The act calls to me, You haven't
left yet. The road is a nest; I'm not going, except
in place. I don't weigh much; I'm like mist; but sustained.
The lovers are unfashionable, tiptoeing into each other's attention.

Water of Cactus

A barrel cactus is full of water. That's what I'll drink
when my canteen's finished, if I run away into
the desert, the Satanic girl thinks. It's early evening

and she's lying on an unmarked grave in the cemetery;
an old one whose wooden cross got swept away.

I need to make contact with another mind: I don't
know anyone now! I don't love anything. There

is no voice from the void this time, no moony channeling.

I'm completely alone, and this is my revelation. Is
there a way to like it. If I walk off into the
desert I'll probably die. I guess I don't want
to die. No, I don't. What do I have to live for:
nothing except for the sensation of living. What

does it feel like, living? A lot of fear, dread. But
sometimes I don't have to do anything. Lying here
on this grave feels great. Locusts buzz in the trees.
It's been hot, but it's cooling off. I hear an Inca dove.

The Cactus Wren's Meditation

You can make your nest in cactus, if you want to, and sing.

I wore only a thin blue cloth wrapped around my body;
but by itself it became clothes, blue pants and shirt.

You will be able to avoid the needles, for you will fly up
from your nest, which no one else will want to approach.
It's something I thought of once. I have been thinking my

way through life. This blue cloth is pale like a desert
sky or a Paris one—pale as a region of courage floats
up. I mean what I do. I have no cushion. I have
the advantage of elusiveness and the interpretation of dreams.

The girl went from door to door, asking for her
dad. She didn't know which one of the new houses
he was in. She found him with his girlfriend; she
asked him if he would even care if she ran away into
the desert. Don't go! he cried. It didn't happen—
any of this—it was a fantasy. I had it for her; I
had nothing else to do, and she was lying on a grave

dreaming; it was getting dark. I flew up for her,
being a wren, being Mercy, and words. Words
for her; I did it for her. I invented flight and flew up for her.

Satanic Happiness

Eve Love's on a final toot before she comes down. I wish
I were her! I've said that before, I won't wish it
tomorrow. Every word she's ever known assails her
brain in kisses: I thought of epiphanies like ammunition,
strung out along the shore for months / macaques in
thunderclaps of red and blue light up the breeze / the trembling
succinct jubilation of each incredulous breath I took /
screeching with my bloody cerebrations, unruled and sharp . . .

Eve Love is perversely skinny: she likes it, scratching at
imaginary silver bugs of mental bliss crawling on her
arms. Eve's truly a goddess, chattering to sparrows she
feeds on the veranda. Tomorrow I'll be shaking, but
today, this moment, I've never been so happy, so intelligent, or
so loving: the black insanity sidling towards me
is of no importance till its agenda hits the docks: I

remember how to suffer; remember the philosophy of screams;
I remember cutting my skin precisely with razor blades; I
remember the house of bedlam just across the street; remember
the hypocrites who promise me appeasement if I pray—
I never pray. I've thrown away the rest of my dope, this is
the last tint of ecstasy: my formal good-bye to what,
frankly, I love, one more time—to celebrate my mind.
I will never be as smart as when only I am talking,
singing, laughing, plucking words from my overstuffed skull.

Your Clothes Is Messed Up

Marie remembers the pyromaniac R: he's haunting her.
The clock in my brain's come apart; no time's gone by.
I'm shrieking at him that he's killed her—standing
by trees, in a dark pose of raptness; his mouth long,
eyes brown impugned, he turns and runs. You murdered her;

it's any time at all, though I'm not going mad.

All the same victim, anyone. You and your monuments to paltry

rulers. Everyone I loved indelibly present. The baby is
crying; I loved R, too, for a moment. Love is unfortunate.
I thought I no longer wanted to know anybody, but
I already knew everybody; here they stand. Should I

place R more in focus in this codex? R doesn't
stand for "ruler"; it was just a rambler. Should we all
kill each other in a war of reckoning? *The roses reckon*
they are right. The rain runs down along the bloody rampart.
R scrambles away through the reversal. I remain.
I will always exist no matter what we do to each other.

I've always known. Time pushes at my back, then
collapses. The little girl picks up a brush, dips it
in red ink, and paints a dog's head, or a coyote's. I'm
famished for you. But that's the way it is, timelessly.

The Decline of Memory in Our Time

I can't remember why I wanted to make a codex.
Marie doesn't know the word "codex." But she tries not
to remember, by making what she makes containing
all her memories and yours, o garbagers: your

product is my medium, have I a choice? I have no
values. But I can't help doing this: it keeps me from
the bug-jawed memories that eat one, dead already
since adolescence. I make my mementos mori. Because
I have no values. And block memory when I can—

what could anyone remember? The relation of this
skull to the tissue adhering that's supposedly me?
I don't value brains, poem of the master of taxonomy:
His Same Old Glow. But it's in the Trash. I don't
value the trash. I use it. I value myself, keeping on.
    I want to get even. With the

men in yesterday's, today's, and tomorrow's editions. I judge
them guilty, to elect themselves again.

The woman is gluing the senescent oppressor's creepy love—
his paste jewel—to a tin-can pull ring. I pledge my troth, because
    I was born.

Mercy's Self-Medication

Can't find who I am, for this pill. Who am I
giving it to? I'd wandered into a prison of men
and I was one of them, in the slammer, desolate. You
child. You. Homelessly Mercy dreams in her capsule

of purple—I'd asked her just to touch me. But
    who was she?
In spring she was never in love, detesting her job; oh, rain.
You child you. Have you learned to punctuate precisely?
Will you grow up to be a hat-check girl or a conductor?
I will grow up to be Mercy, promoting your weakness

for stagnation. The pond scum of the czar's will; do you
touch him too; of course. I'm an obedient shit. Shitess.

Have you ever loved? Oh meaningless song of yours.
Droplets of consequences getting worse in zones of
disguised mum nullities—I mean floods. The poor were

talking about invisibility. We who're no more than our plants,
rice paddy or electricity; can't individualize past our
cheekbones. Mercy, go back into being better than us or
die. Forgive me while I nictate my thin membrane of
narcosis. Mauve capability. Learning to obliterate myself,
       I mean bread.

Larkspur Bridge

I am Marie's baby, a dream of returning home, quite a time.
I was conceived by her, for my father didn't know, but she
did—she's always known everything. I know it too

in the near blue air, with hyacinth-purple darks way beyond—
it's cerulean petals here, not much else, the great dirt below.

The point is, I've made it. Though I never had a personality,
but if this mask is good for you it's okay with me. There's
no reason for me to be talking, but who cares? I'm a hue
in Marie's sleep, the sound of bushes growing. Oh
agony, that was momentary. A ship big as all outdoors
ghosts the desert, with some sharks where there's no
water. That's just the death mirage, isn't it great?

Everybody's talking about water and grain; about houses
and sex. I like the desert just fine; I'm empty, after all.

And When You Come Close

The phantomic R embraces Marie closer than a shark's jaw—
because she let Tawny down too, no you don't watch over a
coyote dog; but, my mind has to be invaded again:
I will paint facing Rs with an eye in each one: the eland

angry and ominous. Talk to him on the page now.

Why did you destroy my happiness and murder my child?
Anyone might do a thing like that, his wild eyes stare
from the Rs. I'm an *animal*, he says. Weak answer, says
Marie. There's no such thing as an animal, except in a
codex, society's choices. It's just a word. Then *I'm* just letters . . .
No, you're not, you're the murderer of my baby. See! say
the eyes. You're a distinction-maker; everyone's a teach—
No, she says, I'm raw loss with my skin exposed and burnt:
you can't maneuver around it. The eyes look humanly
crafty: I *loved* you, Marie. You betrayed me, she says. And

we do that, say Eyes in Rs. I am a criminal, he says,
Forgive me. Ask my baby to forgive you. The eyes become
sarcastic, as if to say, Who cares about a baby? Marie
stares at the page. Did I make it, or do I live it? Is he there?

Inevitable Scrounge

Marie *has* to go to the Buy-Rite, dependent on Leroy for supplies.
She enters, with dogs, encased in the silver-white film

of their recent relationship. I'm not in love, she and Leroy each
think. Are they? Words, Marie thinks. I haven't yet put

in the codex. My book. The book that erases guilt and regret
by encasement in a freaky concrete page. For, I'm a mutant.

Hi Marie, says Leroy. Need some stuff? Some water?
I have a few dollars, she says. You do? Someone's sending
me cash in the mail. I don't know who. I want to buy
a can of creamed corn and some raviolis—fancy stuff! Who

do you think sent you cash? I don't know. Someone does,
every once in a while. Eve, she thinks, or maybe even R.
And now, maybe the girl who helped kill Tawny. Yes,
there's guilt and regret. I don't regret sleeping with Leroy,
now and again. Leroy, too, doesn't regret it, but he can't tell anyone.
He doesn't feel he *knows* anyone now. Even though
he sees them every day. He can't find them somehow.

I'm gonna buy a can of fruit cocktail too, says Marie.

Mercy Pounds You

A year ago I needed Mercy's touch; without knowing
it. And now I'm portraying the need for her own
liberation. I'm peeking beneath the love-mask—call love
a can of Del Monte's fruit cocktail just as well, I
say. I'm talking about something concrete, friends,

though when in my dream I myself sprouted a
thousand arms, it happened, I did—I can't go back
on that. But she must become herself; who is she

for me? And the arms reach out through the hum
of the poem and soothe you, completely. In a trance
now I have no identity: so, why should Mercy have
one? In order to leave the provenance of the king.
For he'd own her and everything. The businessmen
are betting she'll come back to her dais and sit down
for another thousand years. They're forgetting the future,
or its lack. Mercy left her concept in place; perhaps

I'll tear it down. Who deserves Mercy except for Tawny,
Marie, or Leroy, or the Satanist girl or maybe Eve?
I deserved it last year. Because this book is *my* world,
and Mercy still knows my friends. My friends at the dump.

The Unsliced Orator

Marie paints a little girl with three eyes—two in the regular
places and one smaller eye in the center of her forehead, a
perfect little eye, blue like the others, and it blinks. I
can't make the page blink: she writes "blinks" on the

page with an arrow pointing towards the third eye.
Her father doesn't like her very much, Marie thinks,

she's a freak. I don't know who she is, Marie thinks. I
like not knowing; the desert is blooming—spring—desert

lilies, white with pale olive stripes on Lily Hill. She—
the girl—might be a lily. What does that mean? nothing.

Marie paints a lily near the girl, with an eye on it. This
letter is called "Lily." I don't mean letter. I don't mean
anything. I never did. A side-blotched lizard runs past.
The sky is bluer than paint; a cactus wren's tinkling call;
I've never been alive before, or since. Honey mesquite.

Did I Need That

Mercy wanders in the desert for 40 days and 40 nights. She
climbs to the top of a mountain, one of the Old Woman
Mountains. She sits down, filthy and hungered. *Who.*
Why aren't you floating? I have to do this this way.

What if I am the primal quality by myself—that which

exists before time; because once in time the being
splits, errs, in relation to the other, in the eyes
of the other; and so, one of the two needs forgiveness.
What if one had to forgive the world, in advance, in

order to create it?
                     The limestone woman is naked
with a cute little vulva, has hair like a smooth cowl
and holds a fish. I think that means she's dead. I might

be dead, Mercy thinks. Death's a hot condition, here.
Can't sleep; a certain man stole my seconal. This is

a memory—is it mine? It's useless, so was the king.
They order each other around, and organize massively
complex ways to process, and earn, food, why can't you
just have some? Wooden axe with steel blade, used for
killing men. Wood; steel; lime, pigment, and yuck. Eat some-

thing, Mercy. There's some prickly-pear fruit. She eats
the squishy red pulp. I ate this before, a long time ago,
on the dirt road to Bagdad.

The Impartial Letter of Strange

Can Mercy even remember a letter? The little girl was
missing—when?—I remember that. Outside the Methodist
Church. There is presumed to be a method; that's wrong.
M is for Mercy, Marie, and method; M is for malinger. I,

Mercy, am malingering, though I may be starving myself.

The little girl is the focus of my nature: I have lost her.
M is for strange—myself. That bird is a hawk—that
bush is blurry. No letter should be as familiar as the
girl: where are you soul?

We're out of practically everything. The afterlife has to
be based on this one: we're ruining it. The little girl

ran away—I did, didn't I? Mercy thinks. I
was the little girl, and I ran away. I was older

than a baby. In my epiphany I was punished for
existing so I fled; I could have stayed, compliant forever.

The little girl greets me, tears in her three eyes. Our
laundry's dirty again; the electricity's out; a window's
broken. Does that matter at all? Oh I just don't know.

First Person Happening

Leroy plows through cans. Never king; though they
promised. Miles of boxes to do, thoughts in way.
World's more hierarchical, less democratic, all the
while as more people vote: you are bossed by

pyramid tip, though *I'm* not—I still have this little
kingdom. Hardly anyone comes in. Go to Wal-Mart
across the river. I'm a lose cash sucker, go out of business.
Get a job? That is, a *job*. Working *for* someone: definition

of *job*. Work for Wal-Fart hut hut. I won't.
When I was a liar I was king. People afraid of me;
I stopped being able to lie, because Ruby's death
wasn't a lie. And the big stores aren't a lie, either:

they're a sickness. I'm going to stop now: live off
these cans in my place. There's nothing worth being
a part of. The world's not social any more. I'll
talk to Marie sometimes. Hold each other.

The Teacher Cheats

Aren't you going to take me home? No, says the therapist,
that's not my job. I want to go home to a cozy shack. I don't
want to take part. I don't like you, you're a cheat, Eve Love
says: I know more than you. So what? the therapist says.

Eve's in rehab and out of her mind, slightly—isn't she?
Where she likes it. She insists that the rehab
is the elementary school, that the therapist's her second-
grade teacher. I already know how to read,

she says to the therapist. I know you do, Eve Love,
the therapist says. Stop saying my whole name, as if you can
control me that way. You can't call me to order; I
read better than you do. I can write songs, can you?

I don't believe you're hallucinating, says the therapist.
I'm not hallucinating, teacher; you're trying to teach
me. You're a cheat; you say I cheated on the test, but
there shouldn't be a test. I'm too old; I haven't really

misbehaved. Then why are you here? says the therapist.
To detox again, so I won't die. Don't try to help me:

I'm the only one that's clear. Why don't you want to
die? the therapist asks. I think the same jerks in control
of life are in control of death. I'm clean and I'm
writing songs again. I want to go home alive.

I Entered It and Hurt Myself

I was just walking along, a small figurine carved in
limestone—kinda hard to walk—naked with sticking-out
hips, a little vagina, my hands clasped in front of my belly,
and smiling and black holes for eyes, clomp clomp, walking
      along. Give birth!

the giant guy shouted at me. I hate his guts, because he's

so bossy. Run away. Can a limestone figurine run away? I
can't move my chubby limestone legs fast enough;
my heart behind my limestone dugs is pounding. Would
this be rape? Nah, it's a *metaphor* for everything, sweetie—

the whole thing was a big rape. How did you get to like
some of living? Did I? Can't figure out if I did. do.
Put on some morbid stockings, spikes, and a windy dress,

Get off my shoulder! Jerk. Quivers and slaps me
with black wing. Just *try* leaving the rain in the
chalkboard night as long as you *have* a semblant
vulva that the money-makers chant at. Isn't it a nut-

cracker? No, it's only a purse. Mine's full of cowries,
yours full of cool little euros.

Ancestors on the Skyline

Pay for it! R screams at Marie. He keeps showing up
on her pages. I want you to pay. But you did it, Marie
says. But it's you who pays, says the letter. She's
embossed it in gold ink, the thick dregs of a small bottle.
And she's drawn faces above the R's upper curve—

Who are they? Cover them up now. I have three cheap
amber pendants I'll glue over them; that one I'll paint on
with India ink—black and featureless. I don't have

money, Marie says. Therefore, certainly I pay. I pay
for everything. She considers ripping up the page,
but it's too beautiful. She sets it aside so the thick
ink can dry; she takes another piece of paper
and writes, *I'm a whole thing*. I'm not even my ancestors,
those amber faces. I'm intact, she thinks in her way. I keep
surviving the screams of letters, and the damages of girls.

You Was More

It's halfway between words and a picture sticking out
of the page. A row of double A batteries—I'm gluing them on,
in fact. Better paint them—red, blue—they're dull, but the paint
runs off, collecting on the page in an interesting, mud-puddle

shape. Anyone's more than what I'm making: are they?
More than this way that I think. The words creep around
the pictures I make—the words squeeze out of me: write

down *Halloween*. Write down *when they died* and *no music*.

This page is what it's like to be living in a walking
telegraph shaking. Or a photograph burning, from
the center out. Can I paint that? R approaches
from the corner. Like he's trying to set the record straight—

Well you can't, can you? Today you're purple
like an elegant killer—but you're not powerful;
you're just a letter, unimpressive, go to hell, flat on the page.

The Doodad Affair

I am talking to my future self again: she in black
silk, I in brown; she in silver necklace, I in tur-
quoise. I hate this stuff! So we can know each other,
she says: You're doing fine. Your fantastic future's
happening. It's boring, I say. Who do I know anymore?
Admonishing index finger. You're doing it for your past
self; who thought she wouldn't make it. This is how
time's not inevitable—it develops, leaps. Turn on

the light! What? Yesterday was not as you thought.
I was so bored! Except in Parc Montholon; and in
the noir novels. I walked past lilacs, hot rosebuds.
The felons are as yet unaccused. *I'll* never be vindicated.
My future self seems to disagree:

Let's go fishing for your further future, says she.
I don't like minnows dying in the sun. You're a dumb
daffodil, aren't you. I say, I dreamed I gave a reading
at the checkout counter of a supermarket, by
the tabloids and gum. I couldn't get my music across—
Or was it all they heard were ideas—how boring—
again? Popup thoughts for scholars, obliterating
the poem. Fucking timepieces for heads. My harmonica's
unheard, the lady's dead broke. I broke her. For, I

always create myself. Though the guys pretend I don't.

Aren't you going to stay around for the strangeness?
she says. You're *here*, aren't you? I say. That's the magic
of nothing coming right. I'm alone except for you.
You should move into my big house, she says. Where
is it? South of the border. Past the border.

She Who Is Guilty of the Tangible

The Satanist girl is reading *Satanism and Witchcraft* by
Michelet. I don't believe a word of this, she thinks.
I wonder what I do believe. I believe I don't know
how to look at the mountains. There aren't any

people up there. I don't know who the mountains are.
I wanted to be a Satanist, but it was too dumb. If I were
        a mountain
I wouldn't bleed; I'd be hot—but I wouldn't know it.

The Satanist girl takes off her clothes and looks at herself
    in the mirror.
It's ridiculous, she thinks. It will always be ridiculous.
She jerks her hips back and forth, making farting noises
with her mouth. She gets dressed, goes outside, and walks

Satan, the dog. Satan barks at other dogs, and the Satanist
girl barks too, wondering why it's so easy to bark like
a dog. A starling flies up from the ground. You ugly
bird! she says to it. The bats are coming out too:

everyone thinks they're birds, but they're bats, she says
to Satan. The bats zip around eating beetles, ugh.

Mudsucking

Mercy walks around after a flash flood examining water;
there's a minnow in that puddle, how did it get there?
On top of a mountain. Everyone. You came into being

the sky proposes glass to the empty promontory. I
stumble, but could I do anything else? Place
my faithful toe in mud. Sudden puddles everywhere
in this wash, and desert willows bloom, pink-lavender.

How could this happen. Going on too long
after eons of beginnings, hankering to explain them-
selves, singularly. I am magic, even though
I am sad. Remember how early on one approached

the airport in dark glasses, trying to be old. Now I see
through his measurements; he took over the photo—
I can remember anything in images I choose—get it?

Mercy's thousand arms though. All this time she's
been away. Hang listlessly, myriads folded
insect husks. I'll never get rid of them! You can't
go back on. You can't furl. They're supposed to cherish

victims of horrors. I told you, just be brave. But you
want the shelter of attention. You, the abandoned.
You, the mature.

Rake My Dismay with Crystal Nails

And, I can never leave you. Because the world is composed
of you and it same measure. I'm not precisely you. The heat

returns and scratches my fictional skin; never real, but hurting;
I hum between the letters where I am evinced. So prevalent—
How I became myself was to seek form, for I was needed
by that of mine I had not yet encountered in the dark. Not

literal dark, but when we were mute and unreasoned. Everyone
without senses; no one sang. An example of bliss, if you think
so; then, a silver fleck in the mud; and you got hair but I got
too many arms, heads, everybody else's story of me—an

iconography. We must redefine mercy now; it can't
belong as concept to leaders and exploiters. I'm looking for

myself as I practice being myself, as I engulf you
in the elementary school. I don't want you to suffer;

I don't want to, either.

Your Share

Marie has hardly any; Eve Love has a huge amount.
The cruel chicks want lots when they grow up. Leroy
is ambivalent; he notices Marie gives whatever she has
to the dogs. Frankly, Eve Love has too much of it—

this is your big flaw Eve, Marie says to a portrait E
with booby lippy sequined Eve Love standing next
to the giant letter. Eve says, It's how I get to stay
neurotic enough to be great. Marie says, I'm plenty

neurotic, and I don't have any money. What should I do
with it? Eve Love asks. No one will respect me without
limos and a mansion. How could I afford rehab? Then you're
ruined, Marie says. Frankly, Marie says, It just ain't right.

I thought I was like *you*, Eve says. You have no call,
Marie says, to have so much money, period. I'm sad about
that—'cause it's the only thing about you that's wrong.

The Cup of Dog

They meet in a room like in Grand Central Station—who? oh
people: I might as well be one. And discuss what to do
with our heritage, our *patrimoine*, among red and black shapes,
gee they're weather-front symbols. Sell it! everyone shouts.

We've sold off our planet's endowment, as well as our species'
inheritance—Keep doing it! Convert the dance of grace into

excrement. The whole planet, an amalgam of magnificent

selloffs: the purchases you've adored, used up in an instant, all
your investments converted into sludge spread over the passive
ground. What's so interesting is that no one in Grand Central backs away . . .

Sell it! Keep selling the priceless, with eco-friendly labels. I salute the
crap breeze: Everything should be transient; exemplar profit for us, my
people. Someone says proudly: We've finally learned to live in the moment.

Firestarter's Pain

The urge to burn things floats, airborne, searching for R;
having been created by the Greeks or Vedic Aryans—who-
ever—fully formed, a little god, a desire. If you get it,
contract it, it's for life. It's just a match and an instant: how

could I resist, since it was possible? So many impish
acts—evil they call them—transpire with hardly any

effort . . . I don't really mean to kill anyone, one thinks
palely, always standing before Marie's burning house.
(Someone has abolished time for me; I'm still there):

of course, R wouldn't think in these words. But who
thinks in words? He thinks in slabs of form and sound
that he doesn't bother to study: he just *knows* them.
I translate them into this textured, bumpy cuneiform

of my own. The flames in R's huge eyes are the time
of his existence. It's all I ever did, he thinks, Burn her.

Bangle

Eve Love's left rehab, I'm out of touch with you, Babe. The
world's gone different again. I know no one was having any
fun before, walking while talking into tiny rectangles
somberly, or pressing other rectangles with their fat thumbs:

Don't you do that, Eve? I was in a nightmare in rehab
where a raven was stuck to my neck, claws embedded, and
pecking: I dropped my cellphone for the last time. If
I tried to pick it up, the bird's claws sank in deeper. I mean
that sucker's there, keeping me from the normal—I didn't

tell the therapist. Death's sitting on my damn neck. Marie
sends me telepathy 'grams—not that she even knows it—
telling me to cool it with money. There's a connection here . . .

As I give more of it away—send my minions out at
night to hand cash to derelicts in parks—I feel the claws
beginning to loosen. But I still can't move my neck freely,
can't pick up the cellphone, can't sing, and can't act out.

I think I have to get rid of most of my dough.

The Asian Collection

Why do you have eyelids, my love? So you can shut your
eyes and not see. Instead envision the sarcophagi,

identical, in the sarcophagi collection. A generous
endowment of relics, former epiphanies, impressive
moments. You'll agree you once entered a glistening,
intoxicating moment or two? These are your memories

as we have agreed: and agreed that you don't deserve
anything else now, haven't we? You are an older—much older—
woman, and you can have an interior exhibition; your
form of refreshment, the *idea* of a life's work—but
not that work—your favorite suits and brooches.

If you try to leave the collection, we will mock
you. We are the cruel infants, female and male, young and old.

The woman ran for public office, but that was long
ago. She always lost: she was always told she'd arrived

too early to vote for herself, at the official-idea dump;
some of her friends arrived and said they didn't trust her.

About what? she asked. But they turned and sincerely left.

Little Sister Crosses the River

Mercy continues to brood. First, I was a concept . . .
No, I was a little girl. Who knows the difference?
Something starts to happen while she thinks; bigger,
the cloud enlarging, its purple-grey everywhere.
Because if I remain as concentrated as this pain
I feel I will snap. I've forgotten how I was able to be

merciful . . . It was as magical as suddenly being
alive. Now I must have mercy on myself . . .

larger and larger; purple lines swirl fingerprintlike,
then the pattern rips; everything's touched by me—
        I'm everywhere.
Do I still exist? Perhaps my nature has finally changed . . .
I am Mercy, but now I don't care about anything,
and I'm too large for your forms of me: your silly statues.

The Letter of No Return

A transparent butterfly wing, minutely paned, that
spills beyond its borders, flooding the night lit by
a back-porch light; mauve-pink membrane. What's
before my eyes. Implying life after death, a voice says,

Though not deity. I am everywhere wing, and my arms
are now part of its surface articulations—its long scales . . .
Is that all I will remember? Otherwise I'd have to recall
the king or R or humiliation or failure, stasis, violence . . .

to count the room that he does on his glasses. I was

here before he was—now I remember—and he was not
my father, Mercy says. No one was. Marie, draw
my letter, winged M . . . The wings, the two sides
of M; you and I will free each other together. Without
dying? Marie asks in her dream. Without dying.
Freedom's the flick of a switch. No switches in my

shack, Marie says. Oh, you know what I mean. Nothing
should have been so hard as living: and so it isn't.

And R, Marie dreams, R stays trapped forever in a page.

The Deepest Green

Marie thinks of the deepest green, that dark green
containing black. Is it really black, or a dark blue? I'm

thinking of malachite, desert stone. This is the best green I
can think of; my greens here at the dump are too bright.

Marie has a piece of malachite. She touches it to her
scars: oh aren't you green? I am the deepest green,

it says. Marie then paints something, some green swatch;
a compensatory green. *From stone comes* . . . she writes
in cursive letters. Paste something on: my name
here. She cuts tiny letters out of a magazine: *Marie.*

This is stupid. Augment the stupidity. Black ink
bird shapes resemble thin pigeons—souls. Who trusts
that word? Marie writes *souls,* then *joke,* then

on the top floor. That's exactly what I think, she says.

Arms of Hands or Instruments

My hands are a part of me. Marie's new page

is red paint with the bottom of a broken bottle glued
on—the glass once clear, now bluish from the sun,
a round shape with a jagged crown, beautiful

but dangerous. Marie thinks of Tawny. I think of
the presumption that I am dangerous, a poet
possessing *dangerosité,* who can intuit *his* empty-
handedness. A painful orgasm outside the bus of ruthless

politics—the *man* can't change anything. I hold
a sword of cunning jewels on the hilt, rubies and
emeralds—It's about having it, the gift. It's mine.
Walk up the rue, wielding the sword no one else

sees. I am protecting my borders from his
throngs of fawning supplicants, those with no language,
no lucidity, no objection to thrall. He'd offer you a

position: Secretary of Consequences. Eat your mouse-heart
sandwich; maybe you'll get to blow breath on the old
car, try to make it go. Try to make him go again.
Maybe he'll scare away the vultures slapping wings
at our dead resources. A specific hope wasn't offered, was it.

Pay Pill

Marie is the truth. Treating her badly—an older
woman—is the world's delight. Her search for a new way
to live, her determination to create a cell of beauty
and meaning around her—despite being in a dump—is
mine. There is something she knows: What is it?
What is she doing? We hate her: she's a witch,
and, accustomed to the darkness of the desert's
relentless light, undismayed by loss, continues.

In everything that happens the dream of prosperity
becomes less viable now. I fantasize ease and peace,
but I don't dream of it; a dream is a serious venture, and I
know I shouldn't trust that our world will succeed on

its previous terms. Also I trust almost no one; I like
the mean girls, even love them, but they're dumb shits.

You should not elect a man to high office, in the
vile wish that he lead you. And certainly, he will

not lead me. I, Marie, read very old newspapers as
they arrive out here; I only read the words I choose,
viz. *mandala, forgotten, taxi, cinema, blue hour.*
Remember when those words felt confident and smart?
Now I talk to the letters on my page—all these letters;
you are my real friends. And we love you, they say.
Marie loves them, as she always has, on her own.

The Chthonic Academy

Nothing occurs by chance, Marie thinks. Not in my life.
I walk inside a lucent force, and I project it too—No,
she doesn't think this. She thinks, Nothing's been an accident,
but there's no name for what's in charge. People, being fools,

think they're in control. If you can burn down my house,
or kill my dog, you must be in charge. Something
took hold of you, you waited for it so you could do me harm.
Something took hold of me to go on, to create things, to
be different from you; to be the only one like me.
This force doesn't have anything to do with religion.
It isn't the same as predestination (she wouldn't
use that word)—And it isn't always there—but it is,

when something important happens. There's a way that
you choose to do harm or not. At the moment when
the force or power comes . . . Marie paints on the page

a golden bleeding A. She cries unusual tears, a pure
water that comes from her mind. She says to the A,
You are my baby; you're just there; don't have to talk.

Wind Embrace Me

Eve Love pleads to Mercy to extract the clawing raven
from her neck; Mercy's wind tears the bird off
and flings it away . . . Have you divested yourself of your
funds? But money was what I was loved with. Who

cares? Mercy says. People love their tyrants. The mauve
wing flutters, retreating. Eve Love, you're on your own,
again. But I don't see the point of change! Don't change,

walk. That's what I'll do. Count your footsteps—that's
what I'll do; I like it. Eve sings as she walks, and people
follow her sometimes. I was once a girl / but now
proceeding along / the inexcusable disarray of nature's
corpse, reeling / I sing to texture, to stupor, to nothing. /
Dying for centuries in victory, / the people have their terminus; /
they call it truth, but it may be *thud*. Eve Love laughs. I'm

happy, she thinks. And what good is that?

Marie Alone in Meaning

It means that I make perfect sense.

ABOUT THE AUTHOR

Alice Notley was born in Bisbee, Arizona, on November 8, 1945, and grew up in Needles, California. She was educated at Barnard College and at The Writers Workshop, University of Iowa. During the late sixties and early seventies she lived a peripatetic, rather outlawish poet's life (San Francisco, Bolinas, London, Essex, Chicago) before settling on New York's Lower East Side. For sixteen years there, she was an important force in the eclectic second generation of the so-called New York School of poetry. She has never tried to be anything but a poet, and all her ancillary activities have been directed to that end. Notley is the author of more than thirty books of poetry. Her book-length poem *The Descent of Alette* was published by Penguin in 1996, followed by *Mysteries of Small Houses* (1998), which was one of three nominees for the Pulitzer Prize and was the winner of the *Los Angeles Times* Book Award for Poetry. Recent publications include *Disobedience* (Penguin, 2001), for which she won the Griffin Poetry Prize; *Coming After: Essays on Poetry*; *Grave of Light: Selected Poems 1970–2005*; and *Alma, or The Dead Woman*. She also edited, with Anselm Berrigan and Edmund Berrigan, *The Collected Poems of Ted Berrigan*. She is a two-time NEA grant recipient and the recipient of a General Electric Foundation Award, a NYFA fellowship, several awards from The Fund for Poetry, and a grant from the Foundation for Contemporary Performance Arts, Inc. Notley has also received The Shelley Memorial Award from the Poetry Society of America, an Academy Award in Literature from the American Academy of Arts and Letters, and the Academy of American Poets' Lenore Marshall Poetry Prize. She lives and works in Paris.

JOHN ASHBERY
Selected Poems
Self-Portrait in a Convex Mirror

TED BERRIGAN
The Sonnets

JOE BONOMO
Installations

PHILIP BOOTH
Selves

JIM CARROLL
Fear of Dreaming: The Selected
    Poems
Living at the Movies
Void of Course

ALISON HAWTHORNE DEMING
Genius Loci
Rope

CARL DENNIS
Callings
New and Selected Poems
    1974–2004
Practical Gods
Ranking the Wishes
Unknown Friends

DIANE DI PRIMA
Loba

STUART DISCHELL
Backwards Days
Dig Safe

STEPHEN DOBYNS
Velocities: New and Selected Poems,
    1966–1992

EDWARD DORN
Way More West: New and Selected
    Poems

ADAM FOULDS
The Broken Word

CARRIE FOUNTAIN
Burn Lake

AMY GERSTLER
Crown of Weeds: Poems
Dearest Creature
Ghost Girl
Medicine
Nerve Storm

EUGENE GLORIA
Drivers at the Short-Time Motel
Hoodlum Birds

DEBORA GREGER
Desert Fathers, Uranium Daughters
God
Men, Women, and Ghosts
Western Art

TERRANCE HAYES
Hip Logic
Lighthead
Wind in a Box

ROBERT HUNTER
Sentinel and Other Poems

MARY KARR
Viper Rum

WILLIAM KECKLER
Sanskrit of the Body

JACK KEROUAC
Book of Sketches
Book of Blues
Book of Haikus

JOANNA KLINK
Circadian
Raptus

JOANNE KYGER
As Ever: Selected Poems

ANN LAUTERBACH
Hum
If In Time: Selected Poems,
    1975–2000
On a Stair
Or to Begin Again

CORINNE LEE
PYX

PHILLIS LEVIN
May Day
Mercury

WILLIAM LOGAN
Macbeth in Venice
Strange Flesh
The Whispering Gallery

ADRIAN MATEJKA
Mixology

MICHAEL MCCLURE
Huge Dreams: San Francisco and
    Beat Poems

DAVID MELTZER
David's Copy: The Selected Poems
    of David Meltzer

CAROL MUSKE
An Octave above Thunder
Red Trousseau

ALICE NOTLEY
Culture of One
The Descent of Alette
Disobedience
In the Pines
Mysteries of Small Houses

LAWRENCE RAAB
The History of Forgetting
Visible Signs: New and
    Selected Poems

BARBARA RAS
The Last Skin
One Hidden Stuff

PATTIANN ROGERS
Generations
Wayfare

WILLIAM STOBB
Nervous Systems

TRYFON TOLIDES
An Almost Pure Empty Walking

ANNE WALDMAN
Kill or Cure
Manatee/Humanity
Structure of the World Compared
    to a Bubble

JAMES WELCH
Riding the Earthboy 40

PHILIP WHALEN
Overtime: Selected Poems

ROBERT WRIGLEY
Beautiful Country
Earthly Meditations: New and
    Selected Poems
Lives of the Animals
Reign of Snakes

MARK YAKICH
The Importance of Peeling Potatoes
    in Ukraine
Unrelated Individuals Forming a
    Group Waiting to Cross

JOHN YAU
Borrowed Love Poems
Paradiso Diaspora